You are my
Grammar &
Speaking

1 Student Book

Ia**m**books

You are my
Grammar &
Speaking 1 Student Book

Published by

I am Books

#1116, Daeryung Techno Town 12th Bldg.,

14, Gasan digital 2-ro, Geumcheon-gu, Seoul 153-778, Republic of Korea

TEL: 82-2-6343-0999

FAX: 82-2-6343-0995

Visit our website: http://www.iambooks.co.kr

Publishers: Shin Sunghyun, Oh Sangwook

Author: Lucifer EX

Editor: Kim Hyeona

Photo Credits:

Wikipedia (www.wikipedia.org): p. 25 (McDonald's); p. 25 (Pizza Hut) ⓒ Edl; p. 40 (Wayne Rooney) ⓒ Austin Osuide; p. 75 (Nadia Comaneci) ⓒ Dave Gilbert; p. 75 (Neil Armstrong, Thomas Edison); p. 82 (Mother Teresa) ⓒ Túrelio; p. 82 (Beethoven, Alexander Fleming, Florence Nightingale, Alexander Bell, Jacques Cousteau, Pablo Picasso, Walt Disney); p. 82 (Valentina Tereshkova) ⓒ V. Malyshev

Flickr (www.flickr.com): p. 82 (Pablo Picasso) ⓒ Recuerdos de Pandora

All other photos ⓒ imagetoday (www.imagetoday.co.kr)

ISBN: 978-89-6398-091-1 63740

Preface

You are my Grammar & Speaking series is a basic grammar book for beginner learners. There are 61 units in series and each unit is about a different point of English grammar. With the various exercises, interesting photos, and illustrations, students will enjoy English grammar and really can communicate in English, even from the beginning. This book encourages students to speak and write English accurately and fluently by providing them with a solid understanding of English grammar.

This book uses a simple but systematic 4-step approach (Real-life Context, Learn & Practice, Super Writing, Super Speaking) to help young learners master English grammar. This series aims to motivate young learners to learn grammar through various creative tasks such as Super Writing, Super Speaking, and various levels of challenging questions.

You are my Grammar & Speaking series is a useful supplement to any English language courses and is suitable for both classroom teaching and self-study. The series focuses on the key grammar concepts that students need to know for written exercises.

I hope many students will build language and communication skills with this *You are my Grammar & Speaking series*. At the same time, I wish teachers will use *You are my Grammar & Speaking series* as the most appropriate tool for teaching English as a second language. If students learn one language well, they will be able to learn other languages easily. That is why grammar is necessary to learn languages.

I am convinced that through this *You are my Grammar & Speaking series*, a lot of students will definitely have the chance to improve and develop their English grammar skills and abilities.

Thanks and good luck,
Lucifer EX

Structure & Features

You are my Grammar & Speaking series is an easy, friendly, and interesting grammar book series designed for young learners. The series contains interesting photos and illustrations to help students understand grammar points. With this grammar book series, the leaners will learn the rules of essential English grammar with the information about when and how to use them.

• Step 1: *Real-life Context*

The purpose of this part is to introduce students to the grammar point of the unit. This helps students to start the lesson in a very meaningful real-life context with captivating images.

• Step 2: *Learn & Practice*

Vivid photos and illustrations stimulate students' interest and help them understand the meaning and use of grammar. Clear and easy-to-read grammar charts present the grammar structure. The accompanying examples ensure that students understand the grammar point with colorful photos and illustrations.

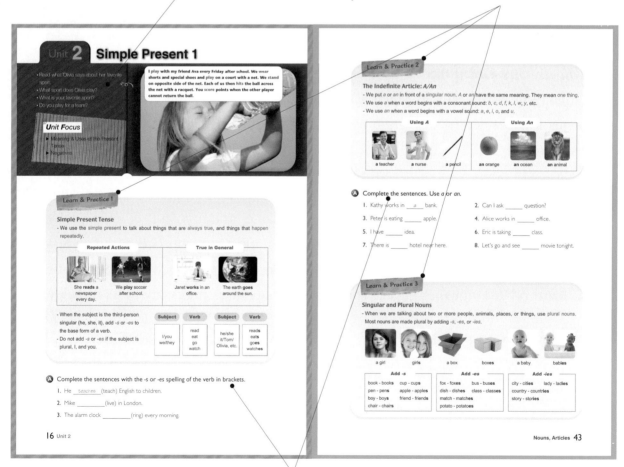

Each Learn & Practice provides various basic exercises and opportunities to practice both the forms and the uses of the grammar structure.

• Step 3: *Super Writing*

A writing activity allows students to interact with one another and further develop their speaking and writing skills. Through these activities, students will have a chance to apply their understanding of the practical uses of grammar.

• Step 4: *Super Speaking*

Super Speaking offers students rich opportunities to apply newly learned grammar to speaking activities. This section will help students to develop speaking skills. Students work in pairs or groups and perform a variety of real-life tasks, progressing smoothly from controlled to free practice. By doing so, the amount of time students speak is increased significantly and cooperation among students is encouraged. In addition, pair and group works help students lessen their communicative stress because it is easier for them to communicate with their peers rather than their teachers.

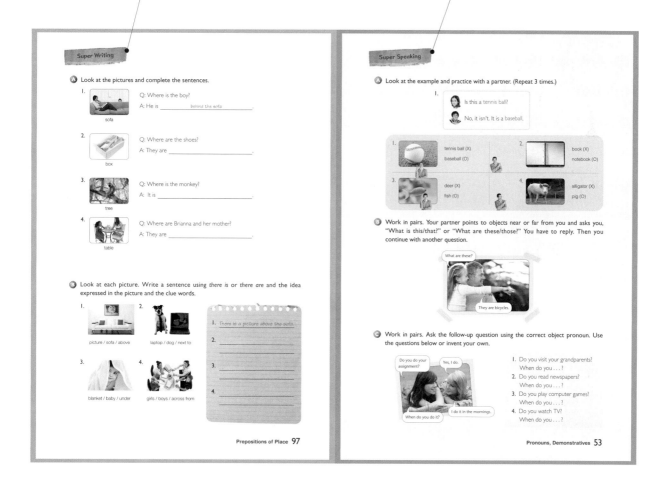

Contents

You are my
Grammar &
Speaking

1 Student Book

books

Unit 1 · Simple Present of Be

Nice to meet you! I'm Kevin and I'm British.

This is Amanda and this is Maria. They're Spanish.

No, we aren't. I'm Spanish and she's Mexican.

• Look at the picture and read the speech bubbles.

Unit Focus

▶ Affirmatives, Negatives, Questions
▶ There Be

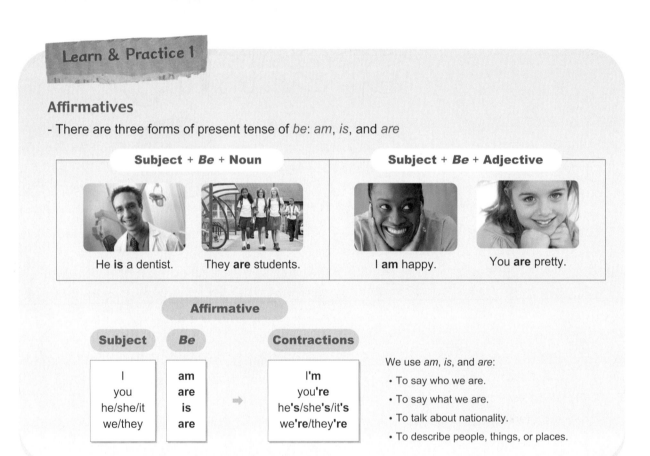

Learn & Practice 1

Affirmatives

- There are three forms of present tense of *be*: *am*, *is*, and *are*

| Subject + *Be* + Noun | Subject + *Be* + Adjective |

He **is** a dentist.   They **are** students.   I **am** happy.   You **are** pretty.

Affirmative

Subject	Be	Contractions
I	am	I'm
you	are	you're
he/she/it	is	he's/she's/it's
we/they	are	we're/they're

We use *am*, *is*, and *are*:
• To say who we are.
• To say what we are.
• To talk about nationality.
• To describe people, things, or places.

A Complete the sentences. Use *am*, *is*, or *are*.

1. My brother and I _are_ good soccer players.

2. It _____ a snake under the tree.

3. Your books _____ on the table.

4. He _____ a police officer.

5. Those people _____ Canadians.

6. I _____ a journalist.

8 Unit 1

Negative of *Be*: *Be* + *Not*

- To make the negative, put *not* after *be*: *am not / is not / are not*

I **am not** happy.
(= I**'m not** happy.)

We **are not** teachers.
(= We**'re not** / We **aren't** teachers.)

They **are not** oranges.
(= They**'re not** / They **aren't** oranges.)

Negative

Pronouns	Be	Not	Contractions with Subject	Contractions with *Not*
I you he/she/it we/they	am are is are	not	I**'m not** you**'re not** he**'s**/she**'s**/it**'s not** we**'re**/they**'re not**	- you **aren't** he/she/it **isn't** we/they **aren't**

∗ *Am not* is always written without contraction.

A Write complete sentences. Use *isn't/aren't*.

1. (your shoes / not / very dirty)   Your shoes aren't very dirty.

2. (they / not / good basketball players) _____

3. (the bank / not / open today) _____

4. (we / not / interested in football) _____

The Verb *Be*: *Yes/No* Questions

- To make *Yes/No* questions, we put the *be* verb before the subject. *Yes/No* questions end with a question mark (?).

- In short answers, we only use *Yes* or *No*. We add *not* if the answer is negative.

Q: **Is he** a field hockey player?
A: **No, he isn't.**
He's an ice hockey player.

Questions	Answers	
Am I . . .?	Yes, you are.	No, you aren't.
Are you . . .?	Yes, I am.	No, I'm not.
Is he/she/it . . .?	Yes, he/she/it is.	No, he/she/it isn't.
Are we/you/they . . .?	Yes, you/we/they are.	No, you/we/they aren't.

A Complete the questions and the answers.

1. _Are_ they Tom's friends?   Yes, _____they are_____ .

2. _____ she an English teacher?   No, _____ .

3. _____ you a student at this school?   Yes, _____ .

4. _____ it a new smartphone?   No, _____ .

Learn & Practice 4

Statements with *There + Be*

- We use *there is/are* to say something exists.
- We use *there isn't/aren't* to say something doesn't exist.

There **is** a student in the library.
There **are** a lot of books in the library.

Q: **Is there** a sofa in the library?
A: No, **there isn't**.

Affirmative		
There	**is**	a book. some water.
There	**are**	some books.

Negative		
There	**isn't**	a book. some water.
There	**aren't**	some books.

Questions		
Is	**there**	a book? some water?
Are	**there**	some books?

A Fill in the blanks with *there is* or *there are*.

1. _____ many different kinds of animals in the zoo.

2. _____ a letter on the table for you.

B Write the complete sentences. (N: negative / Q: question)

1. There is a table in the kitchen.   N: _There isn't a table in the kitchen._

2. There is a telephone on the table.   Q: _____

3. There are buses on the street.   N: _____

4. There are five floors in this building. Q: _____

A Complete the sentences with the correct information.

1.
Bob / a photographer

Bob ___isn't___ a driver.
He is a photographer.

2.
Wesley / a bus driver

Wesley _____ an artist.

_____

3.
Emma / a doctor

Emma _____ a photographer.

_____

4.
the students / from Korea

The students _____ from China

_____

B Make questions and give correct answers.

1. Canada / city → No / a country

Q: _Is Canada a city?_   A: _No, it isn't. It is a country._

2. Africa / city → No / a continent

Q: _____   A: _____

3. Beijing and London / countries → No / cities

Q: _____   A: _____

C Look at the photo and complete the sentences with *there is / there are*.

a laptop	a pen holder	a girl	an apple
some books	glasses	some notebooks	some color pencils

1. *There is a girl at the table.*
2. _____
3. _____
4. _____
5. _____
6. _____
7. _____
8. _____

D Look at Exercise C and write five sentences about things that are in your room.

1. *There is a desk (in my room).*
2. _____
3. _____
4. _____
5. _____

E Read the information about Kelly Smith below. Then complete the questions and answers.

Name: Kelly Smith
Nationality: English
Age: 40
Job: architect
Hobby: watching movies

Olivia: Do you know Kelly Smith?

Peter: Yes, I do. ❶ _____ _____ a lawyer?

Olivia: No, ❷ _____ _____ . She is an ❸ _____ .

Peter: Really? ❹ _____ _____ from Singapore?

Olivia: ❺ _____ , _____ _____ . She ❻ _____ _____ _____ .

A Look at the example and practice with a partner. (Repeat 3 times.)

1.
 Are lemons sweet?

 No, they aren't. They are sour.

1.
lemons / sweet?
→ No / sour

2.
Peter and Karen in Paris / now?
→ No / in Rome

3.
Sunny / a doctor?
→ No / a nurse

4.
 Are there two cakes on the table?

 No, there aren't. There is one cake.

4.
two cakes
→ No / one cake

5.
two women under the tree
→ No / one woman

6.
three birds in the sky
→ No / four birds

B Work in groups. Ask and answer questions. You can look at your book before you speak.

- One student writes down the name of a famous person.
- The other students use words from the vocabulary box and ask questions, as in the example, to guess who the person is.
- The student who guesses correctly continues the game.

A: Is the person a man or a woman?
A: What is he/she?
A: Where is he/she from?

B: A man. / A woman.
B: He's/She's a/an . . .
B: He's/She's from . . .

Vocabulary Box	
Jobs	Countries
actor / actress / artist	Korea / England / the USA
musician / singer / athlete	Italy / China / Japan

Unit 2 Simple Present 1

- Read what Olivia says about her favorite sport.
- What sport does Olivia play?
- What is your favorite sport?
- Do you play for a team?

I **play** with my friend Ava every Friday after school. We **wear** shorts and special shoes and **play** on a court with a net. We **stand** on opposite side of the net. Each of us then **hits** the ball across the net with a racquet. You **score** points when the other player cannot return the ball.

Unit Focus

► Meaning & Uses of the Present Tense
► Negatives

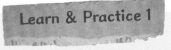

Learn & Practice 1

Simple Present Tense

- We use the simple present to talk about things that are always true, and things that happen repeatedly.

Repeated Actions		**True in General**	
She **reads** a newspaper every day.	We **play** soccer after school.	Janet **works** in an office.	The earth **goes** around the sun.

- When the subject is the third-person singular (he, she, it), add -s or -es to the base form of a verb.
- Do not add -s or -es if the subject is plural, I, and you.

Subject	Verb	Subject	Verb
I/you we/they	read eat go watch	he/she it/Tom/ Olivia, etc.	read**s** eat**s** goe**s** watch**es**

Ⓐ Complete the sentences with the -s or -es spelling of the verb in brackets.

1. He ___teaches___ (teach) English to children.

2. Mike _____ (live) in London.

3. The alarm clock _____ (ring) every morning.

4. They _____ (work) for the same newspaper.

5. Janet _____ (eat) breakfast.

6. We _____ (drive) to work.

Learn & Practice 2

Spelling Rules of the Third-Person Singular

She **is** Emily.
She **eats** breakfast every morning.
She **walks** to school.
She **studies** Korean every day.

- A present-tense verb must agree with its subject.

-s	work → work**s** eat → eat**s** open → open**s** write → write**s**		• Add **-s** to most verbs if the subject is singular.
-es	watch → watch**es** wash → wash**es** fix → fix**es** go → go**es** pass → pass**es**		• Add **-es** to verbs that end with **-ch**, **-sh**, **-x**, **-o**, or **-ss**.
-ies	study → stud**ies** fly → fl**ies** cry → cr**ies**		• If a verb ends in a **consonant + -y**, change the **-y** to **-i** and add **-es**.
Irregular	have → **has**		• No rules

A Look and write the verbs in the present tense.

1. catch → *catches*

2. eat → _____

3. have → _____

4. love → _____

5. speak → _____

6. guess → _____

7. see → _____

8. study → _____

9. fly → _____

B Read and write the correct verb form.

1.

Steve is a police officer.

He _____ a thief. (catch)

2.

Sophia is a teacher.

She _____ students. (teach)

3.

Joseph is a baker.

He _____ cakes. (bake)

Simple Present: Negatives

- Negative statements have *do not* or *does not* before the base verb.
- We use *does not* to make negative sentences in the third-person singular (he, she, it).

We **don't** study Japanese.
We study Korean.

Nancy **doesn't** read a newspaper.
She reads comic books.

The frog **doesn't** run.
It swims in water.

Do Not (= Don't) + Verb

I You We They	**do not** (= **don't**)	study.

Does Not (= Doesn't) + Verb

He She It Olivia	**does not** (= **doesn't**)	study.

- We often use the contractions *don't* and *doesn't* in speaking and informal writing.

A Write *don't* or *doesn't*.

1. He ___doesn't___ play tennis.

2. I _____ drink tea.

3. We _____ watch TV very often.

4. She _____ play the piano very well.

5. Tom _____ like me.

6. Sunny and I _____ have breakfast.

B Complete the negative sentences with the words on the left.

1. (want / not)   Ava is always tired. She ___doesn't want___ to go out.

2. (eat / not)   He eats only chips and pizza. He _____ hamburgers.

3. (drink / not)   She always drinks milk. She _____ coffee.

4. (like / not)   Bob likes to watch sports on TV. He _____ to do exercise.

A Look at the pictures and make sentences.

1.

Maria / brush her teeth / before breakfast

→ Maria brushes her teeth before breakfast.

2.

Edward / read books / on the weekend

→ _____

3.

They / watch DVDs / in the evenings

→ _____

B Complete the sentences using the given information.

1.

drink coffee (X)   drink milk (O)

2.

watch sports on TV (X)   play badminton (O)

3.

like vegetables (X)   like hamburgers (O)

4.

have cats (X)   have a small puppy (O)

1. Jennifer ___doesn't drink coffee___.

She drinks milk. _____

2. Lisa _____.

_____

3. Scott _____.

_____

4. Christina _____.

_____

C Read these sentences and write two correct sentences each time.

1. The sun rises in the west.

   The sun doesn't rise in the west. The sun (= It) rises in the east. _____ (east)

2. The sun goes around the earth.

   _____ (the sun)

3. Penguins live in Africa.

   _____ (the Antarctic)

4. A teacher works in a hospital.

   _____ (a school)

D Choose and complete the sentences. Put *-(e)s* on the verb if necessary.

| make food hot | wash clothes | keep food very cold | copies of papers |
| wash plates and cups | take photographs | keep food cool | |

fridge   camera   photocopier   freezer

washing machine   cooker   dishwasher

1. A dishwasher _____ *washes plates and cups* _____.

2. A cooker _____.

3. Freezers _____.

4. A fridge _____.

5. Washing machines _____.

6. Photocopiers make _____.

7. A camera _____.

A Look at the example and practice with a partner. (Repeat 3 times.)

I.

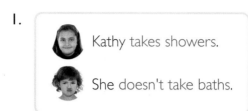

Kathy takes showers.

She doesn't take baths.

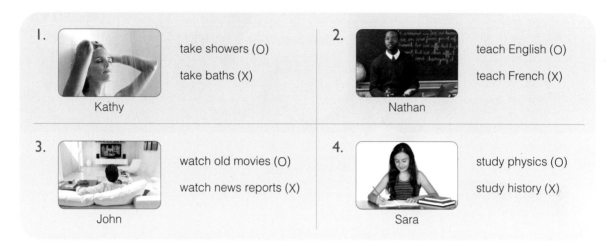

1. Kathy — take showers (O) / take baths (X)

2. Nathan — teach English (O) / teach French (X)

3. John — watch old movies (O) / watch news reports (X)

4. Sara — study physics (O) / study history (X)

B Say five things you and your family do and five things you and your family don't do on different days of the week. Use the words and phrases below or invent your own.

My father plays tennis with me every Saturday.

I go shopping with my mother on Sundays.

Actions	Days of the Week
clean my room	
study English/Korean	Monday
play badminton	Tuesday
go shopping	Wednesday
do my homework	Thursday
meet my friends	Friday
wash the car	Saturday
visit grandparents	Sunday
study math	

Simple Present 2

- Look at the picture and read the speech bubbles.
- Where do you live?
- What does your father do?

Unit *Focus*

▶ Yes/No Questions
▶ Asking Information Questions

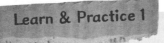

Simple Present: *Yes/No* Questions

- We use *do* or *does* to make questions in the simple present.
- Questions have *do* or *does* before the subject to make a *yes/no* question.

Statements		Questions
She wears glasses.	→	Q: **Does** Sunny wear glasses? A: Yes, she **does**.
She wears glasses all the time.	→	Q: **Does** she wear glasses all the time? A: No, she **doesn't**.

Questions

Do/Does	Subject	Base Verb
Do	I/you/we/they	
Does	he/she/it/Tom/ Mary, etc.	like . . .?

Answers

Yes, I/you/we/they **do**. **No**, I/you/we/they **don't**.

Yes, he/she/it **does**.   **No**, he/she/it **doesn't**.

- We always use the base verb after *do* or *does*. We often use *do* or *does* in short answers to questions.

(A) **Make questions with *do* or *does* and give short answers.**

1. ___Does___ she live with her parents?   Yes, she ___does___ .

2. _____ you like your job?   No, I _____ .

3. _____ your sister visit you very often?   Yes, she _____ .

Simple Present: Information Questions with *Where*

- *Where* asks for information about a place.
- To make an information question, put *where* at the beginning of the sentence.

Statement

Kangaroos live in Australia.

Question

Do kangaroos live in Australia?

Information Question

Q: **Where do** kangaroos live?
A: They live in Australia.

Where	Do/Does	Subject	Base Verb
Where	do	I/you/we/they	study?
	does	he/she/it/Tom, etc.	

Q: **Where do** you live?
A: I live in Seoul.

Q: **Where does** he brush his teeth?
A: He brushes his teeth in the bathroom.

A Circle the correct words.

1. Where (do / does) Anita (work / works)?

2. Where (do / does) you (go / goes)?

3. Where (do / does) he (lives / live)?

4. Where (does / do) it (come / comes) from?

B Complete the sentences with *where do* or *where does*.

1. _____Where does_____ Larry mail a letter?

2. _____ Mary look at paintings?

3. _____ Jimmy wait for the bus?

4. _____ Mrs. Lee get money?

5. _____ they buy a dress?

6. _____ Earth's oxygen come from?

Simple Present: Information Questions with *What*

- The question word *what* asks about information.
- We use a *what* + *do/does* + the subject + the base form of the verb.

Q: **What does** your father do?
A: He teaches history at school.

Q: **What does** he have?
A: He has a kite.

Q: **What do** they like?
A: They like to play soccer.

What	Do/Does	Subject	Base Verb
What	do / does	I/you/we/they / he/she/it	want?

A Read and circle the correct word.

1. What (do / **does**) she want?

2. What (do / does) you like?

3. What (do / does) he have?

4. What (do / does) they eat?

5. What does Bob (buys / buy)?

6. What does it (means / mean)?

B Put the words in the right order to make questions. Add *do* or *does*.

1. (you / want / what / for lunch?) → _What do you want for lunch?_

2. (what / you / do / in your free time?) → _____

3. (what / this word / mean?) → _____

4. (kangaroos / what / eat?) → _____

5. (what / your dad / do / in the morning?) → _____

A Make questions and give answers.

1.

she / drink coffee
→ No / drink tea

Q: *Does she drink coffee?*

A: *No, she doesn't.*

She drinks tea.

2.

Olivia / ride a skateboard
→ No / ride a bicycle

Q: _____

A: _____

_____

3.

Kathy / have a camera
→ No / have a laptop

Q: _____

A: _____

_____

4.

he / do exercise
→ Yes

Q: _____

A: _____

_____

B Look at the pictures and the prompts. Write questions and answers, as in the example.

1.

What / Cindy / do / after school?
→ do one's homework

What does Cindy do after school?

She does her homework.

2.

Where / they / eat lunch / every day?
→ eat lunch at the cafeteria every day

_____

_____

3.

What / Tom / do / in the afternoon?
→ go skateboarding

_____

_____

4.

Where / your parents / go / every Saturday?
→ go to a seafood restaurant

_____

_____

C Read the information about Lucy and Mark. Write questions and answers, as in the examples.

Lucy

LIKES	potato chips, pizza
PLAYS	badminton (afternoon)
GOES	library (weekend)

Mark

LIKES	apple pie, pizza
PLAYS	soccer
GOES	bookstore

1. Lucy / apple pie?

   Does Lucy like apple pie?

   No, she doesn't. She likes potato chips and pizza.

2. Lucy and Mark / pizza?

   _____

   _____

3. Mark / to the library / on the weekend?

   _____

   _____

4. Lucy / soccer / in the afternoon?

   _____

   _____

Lucy

What	
like	cheeseburgers
want	a smartphone

5. Q: *What does Lucy like?*

   A: *She likes cheeseburgers.*

6. Q: _____

   A: _____

Mark

What	
like	music
want	a digital camera

7. Q: _____

   A: _____

8. Q: _____

   A: _____

A Look at the example and practice with a partner. (Repeat 3 times.)

I.

 Do you like sports?

 Well, I prefer music to sports.

1.
   sports   music

2.
   science   arts

3.
   English   Chinese

4.

 What does Korean food taste like?

 Some dishes are spicy, while others are savory.

6.

 Where do you usually go out for dinner?

 McDonald's. That place is famous for its hamburgers.

4.  Korean
   spicy, savory

6.  McDonald's
   hamburgers

5.  Japanese
   mild, bland

7.  Pizza Hut
   pizzas

B Work with a partner to make conversations. Begin your answer with *no*.

E.g.
the children / walk to school every day
→ No / take the school bus

Jane / watch TV in the morning
→ No / read a newspaper

Jason / play computer games
→ No / send emails

Do the children walk to school every day?

No, they don't. They take the school bus. Your turn now.

they / take the bus to work every day
→ No / ride their bicycles to work every day

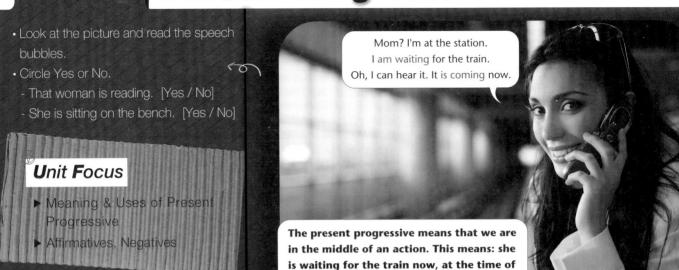

Unit 4 Present Progressive 1

- Look at the picture and read the speech bubbles.
- Circle Yes or No.
  - That woman is reading. [Yes / No]
  - She is sitting on the bench. [Yes / No]

Unit Focus
▶ Meaning & Uses of Present Progressive
▶ Affirmatives, Negatives

Mom? I'm at the station.
I am waiting for the train.
Oh, I can hear it. It is coming now.

The present progressive means that we are in the middle of an action. This means: she is waiting for the train now, at the time of speaking. The action is not finished.

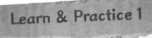

Learn & Practice 1

Present Progressive: Affirmative Statements

- We use the present progressive to talk about something happening now.

Nancy **is drinking** orange juice.
She **is wearing** a hat.
She **is looking** at something.

The students **are studying** in the library.
They **are reading**.

- We form the present progressive with the present tense of the verb *be* and the main verb with the ending *-ing*.

Subject	Be Verb	Verb + -ing
I	am	
He/She/It	is	read**ing**.
You/We/They	are	

Ⓐ Make affirmative sentences in the present progressive.

1. The lesson ___is starting___ (start) now.
2. It _____ (rain) now.
3. You _____ (talk) too fast.
4. Bill _____ (cook) dinner now.
5. He _____ (work) in the garden.
6. Children _____ (play) in the park.

Present Progressive: Spelling Rules of Verb-*ing*

Most Verbs: + -*ing*

talk	→ talk**ing**	go	→ go**ing**
walk	→ walk**ing**	play	→ play**ing**
drink	→ drink**ing**	enjoy	→ enjoy**ing**
sleep	→ sleep**ing**	draw	→ draw**ing**

• Add -*ing* to most verbs.

Remove -*e* + -*ing*

come	→ com**ing**	smile	→ smil**ing**
dance	→ danc**ing**	come	→ com**ing**
make	→ mak**ing**		
write	→ writ**ing**		

• If a verb ends in a **vowel + consonant + -e**, remove -*e* and add -*ing*.

Double Consonant + -*ing*

sit	→ sit**ting**	swim	→ swim**ming**
run	→ run**ning**	get	→ get**ting**
cut	→ cut**ting**		

• If a verb ends in a **vowel + consonant**, double the consonant and add -*ing*.

A Add -*ing* to the verbs below and put them in the correct column.

sit	get	take	play	dance	study
begin	stop	write	clean	visit	make

walk → walking	ride → riding	cut → cutting
visiting		

B Find and correct the mistakes.

1. I am <u>siting</u> in front of the window now.　　→　　_sitting_

2. I am lookking out of the window.　　→　　_____

3. People are walkking in the street.　　→　　_____

4. A girl is rideing her bicycle.　　→　　_____

5. A little boy is eatting ice cream.　　→　　_____

Present Progressive: Negatives

- To make the negative of the present progressive, we use *not* after the verb *be*.

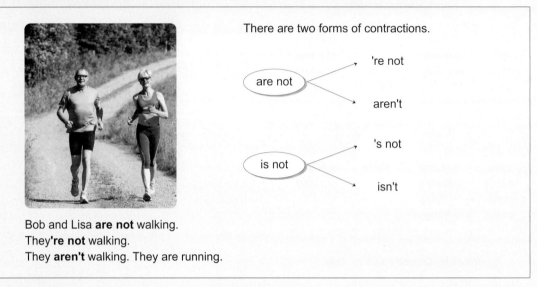

There are two forms of contractions.

are not → 're not / aren't

is not → 's not / isn't

Bob and Lisa **are not** walking.
They**'re not** walking.
They **aren't** walking. They are running.

I	**am not** ('m not)	
He/She/It	**is not** ('s not / isn't)	**-ing.**
You/We/They	**are not** ('re not / aren't)	

A Write the negative form of the sentences with two forms of contractions.

1. She is working.   _She's not working._ / _She isn't working._

2. I am sitting in a cafe.   _____ / _____

3. It is snowing.   _____ / _____

4. We are making dinner.   _____ / _____

5. They are coming now.   _____ / _____

6. Ann is reading a newspaper.   _____ / _____

7. He is studying at home.   _____ / _____

A Put the verb into the correct form.

1. Please don't make so much noise. My baby _____is sleeping_____. (sleep)

2. Let's go out now. It _____ (not / snow) anymore.

3. Please be quiet. I _____ (try) to concentrate.

4. You _____ (make) a lot of noise. Can you be a little bit quieter?

5. Listen! Can you hear those people next door? They _____ (yell) at each other again.

6. She _____ (not / work) this week. She's on vacation.

B Look and complete the sentences.

1.

watch TV (X)
listen to music (O)

She _____isn't watching TV_____.
She _____is listening to music_____.

2.

walk (X)
ride their bicycles (O)

They _____.
They _____.

3.

study in the library (X)
walk to school (O)

The students _____.
They _____.

4.

run (X)
swim in a pool (O)

Linda _____.
She _____.

C Look at the pictures and use the verbs in the box to say what the women are doing.

> brush   get up   open   go   drink   read   wash   brush

1. *She is getting up.*
2. _____ her face.
3. _____ her teeth.
4. _____ coffee.
5. _____ the newspaper.
6. _____ her hair.
7. _____ the door.
8. _____ to work.

1. 2. 3.
4. 5. 6.
7. 8.

D Look at the photo and read the statements. Write the correct negative and affirmative sentences.

stand in the street
a book
look at the man
her phone
the sun / shines

1. The man and the woman are sitting in a cafe.
   The man and the woman aren't sitting in a cafe.
   They are standing in the street.

2. The man is speaking on the phone.
   _____
   _____

3. The man is holding a newspaper.
   _____
   _____

4. The woman is looking at the book.
   _____
   _____

5. The woman is holding a suitcase
   _____
   _____

6. It is snowing.
   _____
   _____

A Look at the example and practice with a partner. (Repeat 3 times.)

1.

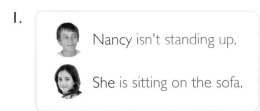

Nancy isn't standing up.

She is sitting on the sofa.

1.

Nancy

stand up (X)

sit on the sofa (O)

2.

Lucy

watch the news (X)

talk on the phone (O)

3.

Kelly

wash her face (X)

brush her teeth (O)

4.

Christina

work on her computer (X)

read a magazine (O)

B Describe two of the people in the picture. Say five sentences about what they are wearing and what they are doing. Use the phrases below.

The woman is speaking on the phone.

The man is wearing a striped shirt.

hold her phone

wear blue jeans

sit on a chair

look at his laptop

look at her credit card

work on his laptop

wear a white dress

hold her credit card

A Complete the answers.

1. Are you hungry? (thirsty)

No, I'm not hungry. _____   I'm thirsty. _____

2. Are they good soccer players? (tennis players)

_____   _____

3. Is he an astronaut? (a firefighter)

_____   _____

4. Is the book expensive? (cheap)

_____   _____

B Write the correct forms to describe the pictures.

1.

It rains every day.

It _____ now.

2.

Kelly plays the guitar every day.

She _____ the guitar now.

3.

They swim in the pool every day.

They _____ in the pool now.

C Write the verbs in the simple present.

1. Megan _____ (speak) four languages.

2. The Art Museum _____ (close) at 6 o'clock in the afternoon.

3. Becky is a teacher. She _____ (teach) mathematics to young children.

4. Heng _____ (live) in Beijing, China.

5. We both _____ (have) dark brown hair and green eyes.

D **Look at the answers and write the correct questions.**

- Do you like movies?
- Does he have a new car?
- Does Susan walk to school?
- Do they love her?

1. _____ → Yes, he does.

2. _____ → No, they don't.

3. _____ → No, I don't.

4 _____ → Yes, she does.

E **Read and Write.**

1.

   I don't wash my face.
   I brush my teeth.

   Nancy _____*doesn't wash her face*_____ .

   She _____*brushes her teeth*_____ .

2.

   I don't drink coffee.
   I drink milk every day.

   Jeff _____ .

   He _____ .

3.

   I don't play tennis.
   I play badminton every day.

   Olivia _____ .

   She _____ .

F **Make negative sentences in the present progressive.**

1. I / not ask for / a lot of money. → *I'm not asking for a lot of money.*

2. She / not listen / to me. → _____

3. It / not rain / now. → _____

4. She / not wear / a coat. → _____

5. We / not enjoy / this film. → _____

6. You / not eat / much / these days. → _____

Unit 5 Present Progressive 2

- Look at the picture and read the speech bubbles.
- Circle Yes or No.
  - Is the woman talking on the phone? [Yes / No]
  - Is she wearing earrings? [Yes / No]

Unit Focus

▶ Yes/No Questions
▶ Future Plans
▶ Information Questions

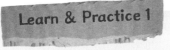

Present Progressive: *Yes/No* Questions

- To make a *yes/no* question, we put *am*, *is*, or *are* before the subject.

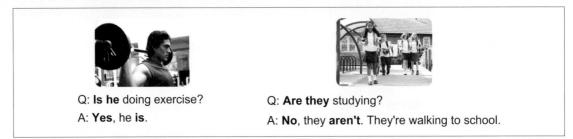

Q: **Is he** doing exercise?
A: **Yes**, he **is**.

Q: **Are they** studying?
A: **No**, they **aren't**. They're walking to school.

- We often use short answers in speaking and informal writing. Don't use contractions in affirmative short answers.

Be Verb	Subject	Verb + *-ing*?
Am	I	
Is	he/she/it/Tom, etc.	study**ing**?
Are	you/we/they	

Q: **Is he** dancing?
A: **Yes**, he **is**. / **No**, he **isn't**.

Q: **Are the boys** cleaning the house?
A: **Yes**, they **are**. / **No**, they **aren't**.

A Complete the questions and answers.

1. ___Is___ she ___wearing___ (wear) a hat?   No, ___she isn't___.
2. _____ your sister _____ (study)?   Yes, _____.
3. _____ David _____ (cook)?   No, _____.
4. _____ the children _____ (do) their homework?   Yes, _____.

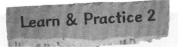

Present Progressive as a Future Tense

- We use the present progressive to talk about future plans.

Now	Future Plan
Those girls **are having** lunch now.	George **is flying** to Seoul in two hours. He's at the airport now.

- We often use a time expression with the present progressive.

I **am seeing** John **this evening**.   Kevin **is meeting** the boss **in 30 minutes**.

A Complete the sentences using the present progressive and check when they happen.

	Now	Future Plan
1. We _____ (go) camping tomorrow.	☐	☐
2. He _____ (take) a walk in the park.	☐	☐
3. Jim's parents _____ (take) him to Texas next week.	☐	☐
4. My favorite TV program _____ (start) in a minute.	☐	☐
5. We _____ (rush) to the airport to meet Mr. Smith.	☐	☐
6. She _____ (have) dinner with Bob on Friday.	☐	☐
7. Water _____ (boil). Can you turn it off, please?	☐	☐
8. Alex _____ (get) married next month.	☐	☐

Present Progressive: Information Questions

- To make an information question in present progressive, we put *what* or *who* before the verb *be*.

Statement

Paul is playing the drums.

Question

Is Paul playing the drums?

Information Question

Q: **What is** Paul do**ing**?
A: He is playing the drums.

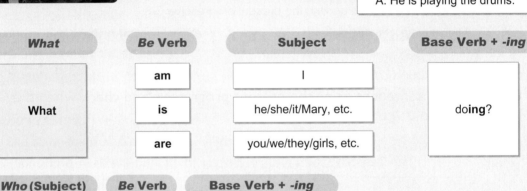

What	Be Verb	Subject	Base Verb + -ing
What	am	I	doing?
	is	he/she/it/Mary, etc.	
	are	you/we/they/girls, etc.	

Who (Subject)	Be Verb	Base Verb + -ing
Who	is	studying? cooking? dancing?

Q: **Who is** cook**ing**?
A: My father is cooking.
Q: **Who is** setting up a tent?
A: My mother is setting up a tent.

Ⓐ Complete the information questions and answers.

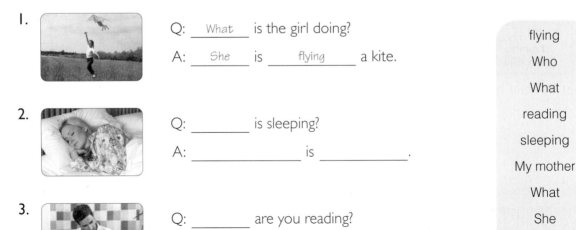

1. Q: __What__ is the girl doing?
   A: __She__ is __flying__ a kite.

2. Q: _____ is sleeping?
   A: _____ is _____.

3. Q: _____ are you reading?
   A: _____ am _____ a science magazine.

flying
Who
What
reading
sleeping
My mother
What
She
I

A Look at the pictures and write questions.

1.

stand next to a horse

Q: Is she standing next to a horse? _____

A: Yes, she is.

2.

wash his dad's car

Q: _____

A: Yes, he is.

3.

paint the house

Q: _____

A: Yes, they are.

B Write about what Jane is doing on Saturday. Use the present progressive with future meaning, as in the example.

9:00 play badminton with her father

11:00 meet Bob and Laura at the department store

12:00 have lunch with her friends

2:00 go to the movie theater with her mother

4:00 study in the library

6:00 eat dinner with her family

8:00 do her math homework

1. At 9:00 she is playing badminton with her father. _____

2. _____

3. _____

4. _____

5. _____

6. _____

7. _____

C Make questions and answers to describe the pictures.

1.

she / watch TV
→ No / listen to music

1. Q: Is she watching TV?
   A: No, she isn't.
   She is listening to music.

2. Q: _____
   A: _____
   _____

3. Q: _____
   A: _____
   _____

4. Q: _____
   A: _____
   _____

2.

they / learn science
→ No / learn history

3.
he / read a book
→ No / work on his laptop

4.
he / drink tea
→ No / wash the dishes

D Make questions or answers using the words given.

1.
My dad

2.

play the guitar

3.
Maria

4.

buy clothes

5.
Daniel

6.

taste the soup

1. Q: Who is driving the car?
   A: My dad is driving the car.

2. Q: What is she doing?
   A: _____

3. Q: _____
   A: Maria is waiting for the train.

4. Q: What is she doing?
   A: _____

5. Q: _____
   A: Daniel is sleeping in the office.

6. Q: What is the cook doing?
   A: _____

A Look at the example and practice with a partner. (Repeat 3 times.)

1.

 Is she waiting for the bus?

 No, she is taking the subway.

1.

she

wait for the bus (X)

take the subway (O)

2.

he

take off the clothes (X)

get dressed (O)

3.

they

walk on the road (X)

ride their bicycles (O)

4.

they

work very hard (X)

have a wonderful holiday (O)

5.

 What is she doing?

 She is eating a hamburger.

5.

she / eat a hamburger

6.

they / take Taekwondo lessons

7.

he / play volleyball

B Work in pairs. Ask each other about your plans for the summer. Use the present progressive and some of the verbs in the box.

travel	visit
go	stay
fly	meet
do	start

What are you doing this summer?

I'm traveling to France in the summer.

Your turn to ask!

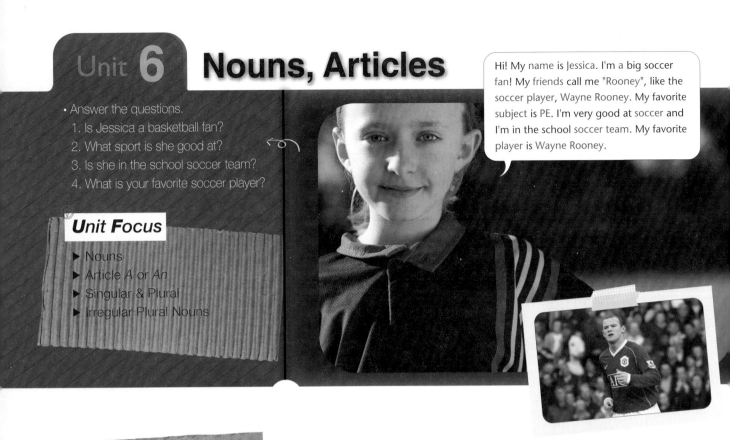

Unit 6 Nouns, Articles

Hi! My name is Jessica. I'm a big soccer fan! My friends call me "Rooney", like the soccer player, Wayne Rooney. My favorite subject is PE. I'm very good at soccer and I'm in the school soccer team. My favorite player is Wayne Rooney.

- Answer the questions.
  1. Is Jessica a basketball fan?
  2. What sport is she good at?
  3. Is she in the school soccer team?
  4. What is your favorite soccer player?

Unit Focus

▶ Nouns
▶ Article *A* or *An*
▶ Singular & Plural
▶ Irregular Plural Nouns

Learn & Practice 1

Nouns

- Nouns are divided into common nouns and proper nouns. Common nouns are words for people, animals, places, or things. Most nouns are common nouns.
- Proper nouns are the names of specific people, places, or things. They always begin with a capital letter.

Common Nouns: teacher, dog, elephant, park, bottle, girl, car, library

Proper Nouns: Olivia, Santa Claus, Egypt, Paris, Korean, Lotte World

---

A Check the common noun, circle the proper noun, and write.

	Common Noun	Proper Noun
1. (Nancy) is a teacher.	teacher	Nancy
2. Chicago is a city		
3. The Nile is a river.		
4. Yonsei University is a school.		

The Indefinite Article: *A/An*

- We put *a* or *an* in front of a singular noun. *A* or *an* have the same meaning. They mean one thing.
- We use *a* when a word begins with a consonant sound: *b, c, d, f, k, l, w, y*, etc.
- We use *an* when a word begins with a vowel sound: *a, e, i, o*, and *u*.

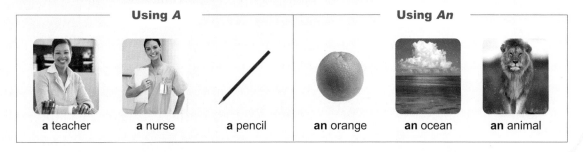

Using *A*	Using *An*
a teacher **a** nurse **a** pencil	**an** orange **an** ocean **an** animal

A Complete the sentences. Use *a* or *an*.

1. Kathy works in ___*a*___ bank.

2. Can I ask _____ question?

3. Peter is eating _____ apple.

4. Alice works in _____ office.

5. I have _____ idea.

6. Eric is taking _____ class.

7. There is _____ hotel near here.

8. Let's go and see _____ movie tonight.

Singular and Plural Nouns

- When we are talking about two or more people, animals, places, or things, use plural nouns. Most nouns are made plural by adding *-s*, *-es*, or *-ies*.

a girl	girl**s**	a box	box**es**	a baby	bab**ies**

Add *-s*	Add *-es*	Add *-ies*
book - book**s** cup - cup**s**	fox - fox**es** bus - bus**es**	city - cit**ies** lady - lad**ies**
pen - pen**s** apple - apple**s**	dish - dish**es** class - class**es**	country - countr**ies**
boy - boy**s** friend - friend**s**	match - match**es**	story - stor**ies**
chair - chair**s**	potato - potato**es**	

A Write the plural of the following words.

1. box → *boxes*
2. boy → _____
3. city → _____
4. fox → _____
5. tool → _____
6. bench → _____
7. bus → _____
8. potato → _____
9. ship → _____
10. country → _____
11. lady → _____
12. bike → _____

Learn & Practice 4

Irregular Plural Nouns

- Some nouns change spelling from the singular form to the plural. We need special forms.

Plural	women	children	teeth	mice / fish
Singular	a woman	a child	a tooth	a mouse / a fish

Plural	men	feet	geese / sheep / deer	people
Singular	a man	a foot	a goose / a sheep / a deer	a person

A Look at the pictures and complete the sentences.

1. 2. 3. 4. 5.

1. Sarah is brushing her ____*teeth*____.

2. There are a lot of _____ in the river.

3. There are two _____ at the bus stop.

4. Jane has two _____.

5. Two _____ are sitting on a sofa.

A Write the plural forms in the correct places.

apple	glass	fish	church	table	dress	tomato
woman	chair	person	story	man	boat	bus
lady	city	ship	country	dictionary	goose	

Add -s	Add -es	Add -ies	Irregular
apples	glasses		

B Look at the pictures and write the answers.

1.

Q: What is it?
A: It is an elephant.

2.

Q: Are they men?
A: No, they aren't. _____

3.

Q: Is there a child?
A: No, there isn't. _____

4.

Q: What is it?
A: _____

5.

Q: What are these?
A: _____

6.

Q: What is it?
A: _____

C Look at the pictures and make sentences with *a* or *an*.

1.
taxi driver

2.
auto mechanic

3.
architect

4.
English teacher

5.
photographer

6.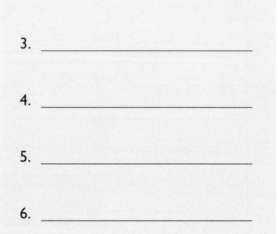
electrician

1. He is a taxi driver. _____

2. _____

3. _____

4. _____

5. _____

6. _____

D For each sentence, change the singular subject and verb to the plural.

1. The pencil is on Maria's desk. → The pencils are on Maria's desk. _____

2. The baby is in the crib. → _____

3. The woman is living in London. → _____

4. The tomato from the store looks yummy! → _____

5. The city looks great after the clean-up effort. → _____

6. The mouse is coming to us. → _____

7. The man is looking at me. → _____

A Look at the example and practice with a partner. (Repeat 3 times.)

1.

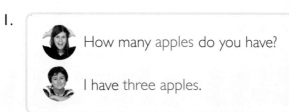

How many apples do you have?

I have three apples.

1. apple / apple (3)

2. egg / egg (4)

3. puppy / puppy (2)

4. sheep / sheep (5)

5. potato / a lot of, potato

B The teacher divides the class into two groups and says a noun. The groups in turn have to say the plural of each word. Each correct answer gets 1 point. The group with the most points is the winner.

child   woman   orange   apple   hand

girl   tooth   foot   man   fish

banana   goose   deer   boy and woman

desk   mouse   page   exercise   city

girl and man   friend   glass   fox

box   bench   baby   lady   story

dish   person   sheep   country   bus

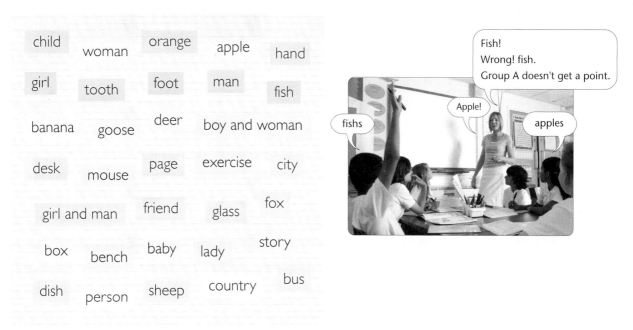

Fish!
Wrong! fish.
Group A doesn't get a point.

Apple!

fishs

apples

Unit 7 Pronouns, Demonstratives

- Answer the questions.
  1. Does Tina play the guitar?
  2. Does Olivia play the saxophone?
  3. What do you want to be when you grow up?

Unit Focus
► Subject Pronouns
► Object Pronouns
► Demonstratives

Hello, I'm Tina. What's your name?

I'm Olivia. I have got a band. I play the guitar. I like it very much.

I play the saxophone. My parents tell me: "Don't play music all the time!", but I tell them, "I want to be a musician."

Look at that woman! She is our teacher.

Learn & Practice 1

Subject Pronouns

- *A* pronoun is a word that takes the place of one or more nouns. A subject pronoun is used as the subject of a sentence.

Singular	Plural
I	we
you	you
he	they
she	
it	

- We use **he** for a boy and a man.
- We use **she** for a girl or a woman.
- We use **it** for an animal, a thing, or a place.
- We use **they** for people, animals, things, or places.
- We use **you** in the singular and plural for both forms.

The man is Dennis.
= **He** is a dentist.

The black car is fast.
= **It** is fast.

Mike and I are friends.
= **We** have got a band.

The pencils are colorful.
= **They** are colorful.

Ⓐ Underline the subjects. Then rewrite the sentences with the correct pronouns.

1. Sunny is a doctor. → _____She is a doctor._____

2. Lisa and I dance well. → _____

3. Roy and Ron are twins. → _____

4. The puppy is white. → _____

5. The bananas are yellow. → _____

6. The comic books are on the table. → _____

Object Pronouns

- We use object pronouns as objects of verbs. They always go after verbs.
- Object Pronouns can be used after a preposition.

Singular	Plural
me	us
you	you
him	them
her	
it	

I like Kathy.
= I like **her**.

Tom is looking at the cars.
= He is looking at **them**.

Kevin likes riding my bicycle.
I sometimes lend **it** to **him**.

Mother loves her children.
= She loves **them**.

A Circle the correct pronouns.

1. We meet (them / they) at a restaurant.

2. Jimmy likes (her / she).

3. My mom is waiting for (we / us).

4. Lisa has a book. She bought (it / them).

5. She is looking at (me / I).

6. Ava loves (he / him) very much.

B Put in the pronouns.

1. Who is that woman? Why are you looking at ___her___?

2. You and I work well together. _____ are a good team.

3. I've got a bit of a problem. Could _____ help _____, please?

4. "Do you know that man?" "Yes, I work with _____.

5. "What shall I do with these letters?" "Just put _____ on the table."

6. "Can I have John's address?" "I'll give _____ to you this afternoon."

7. "Where are your glasses?" "I've lost _____."

Demonstratives

- We use *this* (singular) / *these* (plural) to point to people, things, and animals near us.
- We use *that* (singular) / *those* (plural) to point to people, things, and animals far away from us.

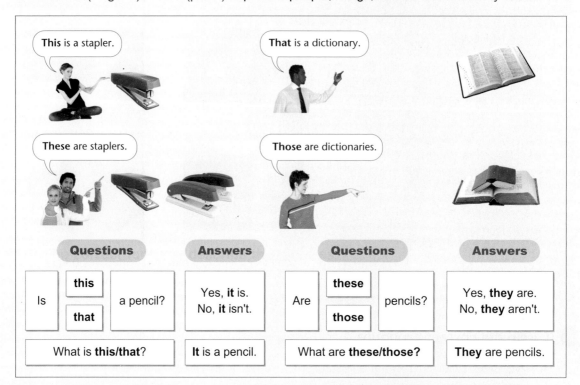

- We use *this/that* and *these/those* in questions. We answer these questions with it or they.

A Complete the sentences, as in the example.

1.

_____This is_____ a pencil and _____that is_____ a cheetah.

2.

_____ a pig and _____ pencils.

B Look at the pictures and fill in the blanks.

1.

Q: Is _____this_____ an apple?

A: No, _____it isn't_____ . It is an orange.

2.

Q: Are _____ paintings?

A: No, _____ . They are notebooks.

A Correct the errors.

1. I don't know that woman. Do you know she?

→ _____

2. Where is my T-shirt? I need them.

→ _____

3. My sisters are going to the movies. I want to go with us.

→ _____

4. I need this smartphone. Give them to me.

→ _____

B What is in the classroom? Write sentences using this/that or these/those.

desk	notebook	schoolbag	painting	computer
skateboard	paper bin	sofa	clock	

This is my classroom.

1. _____ These are computers. _____   2. _____ This is a desk. _____

3. _____   4. _____

5. _____   6. _____

7. _____   8. _____

9. _____   10. _____

C Read the following passage. Write the missing subject and object pronouns in the blank spaces.

My name is James. ___I___ have two brothers.
_____ are both older than _____. Sometimes
they take me to the park and _____ play
basketball together. I like playing basketball with
_____. we are going to the park today. Would
you like to come with _____? _____ can all
play together. Afterwards, we can come to my
house if _____ want to. I think _____ will like
my mom. _____ is very funny and _____ will
make delicious cookies. Do you like _____?

D Look at the pictures and complete the sentences.

1. ___Is that___ a pencil?   No, it isn't.

    It is a schoolbag.

schoolbag

2. _____ lemons?   _____

    _____

orange

3. What _____?   _____

horse

4. _____ a game player?   _____

    _____

MP3 player

A Look at the example and practice with a partner. (Repeat 3 times.)

1.

Is this a tennis ball?

No, it isn't. It is a baseball.

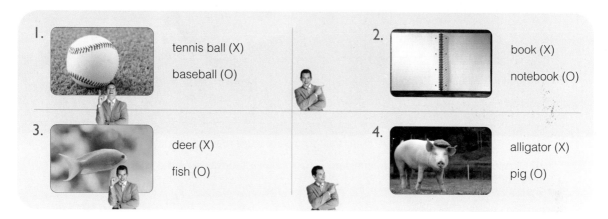

1. tennis ball (X)
baseball (O)

2. book (X)
notebook (O)

3. deer (X)
fish (O)

4. alligator (X)
pig (O)

B Work in pairs. Your partner points to objects near or far from you and asks you, "What is this/that?" or "What are these/those?" You have to reply. Then you continue with another question.

What are these?

They are bicycles.

C Work in pairs. Ask the follow-up question using the correct object pronoun. Use the questions below or invent your own.

Do you do your assignment?

Yes, I do.

When do you do it?

I do it in the mornings.

1. Do you visit your grandparents?
When do you . . . ?
2. Do you read newspapers?
When do you . . . ?
3. Do you play computer games?
When do you . . . ?
4. Do you watch TV?
When do you . . . ?

Unit 8 Possessives

• Answer the questions.
1. Whose laptop computer is that?
2. What are the students doing in the picture?
3. What is your school teacher's name?

Unit Focus

▶ Possessive Adjectives
▶ Possessive Nouns
▶ Possessive Pronouns
▶ Questions with *Whose*

Learn & Practice 1

Possessive Adjectives

- We use possessive adjectives before nouns to show that something belongs to someone.

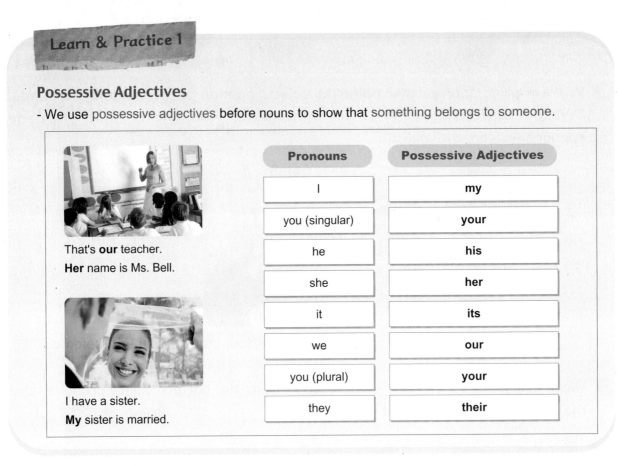

That's **our** teacher.
Her name is Ms. Bell.

I have a sister.
My sister is married.

Pronouns	Possessive Adjectives
I	**my**
you (singular)	**your**
he	**his**
she	**her**
it	**its**
we	**our**
you (plural)	**your**
they	**their**

Ⓐ Complete the sentences with *my, our, her, his, your, their,* or *its.*

1. Ava is doing ___her___ homework.

2. Do you live with _____ parents?

3. We love _____ new apartment.

4. The children are with _____ grandfather.

5. He's looking for _____ shoes.

6. I like visiting _____ friends on the weekend.

7. The street is around here somewhere, but I've forgotten _____ name.

Possessive Nouns

- Possessive nouns show belonging.
- We use an apostrophe (') + -s to a singular noun or an irregular plural noun.
- We use only an apostrophe (') to a plural noun ending in -s.

I'm wearing my roommate's shoes.
(The shoes belong to my roommate.)

Joe	→	Joe's hat
friend	→	friend's bag
father	→	father's jacket
women	→	women's restroom
parents	→	parents' anniversary
children	→	children's uniforms

A Write the correct possessive form.

1. friend name → _friend's name_
2. dog tail → _____
3. women shirts → _____
4. Jane phone → _____
5. boys skateboards → _____
6. teachers room → _____

Possessive Pronouns

- A possessive adjective has a noun after it: your dog, my book, etc.
- A possessive pronoun does not have a noun after it: yours (= your dog), mine (= my book), etc.

That is your backpack.
= That is **yours**.

This is my smartphone.
= This is **mine**.

Is that her bicycle?
= Is that **hers**?

That is their house.
= That is **theirs**.

Possessive Pronouns

my book	= mine
your book	= yours
his book	= his
her book	= hers
their book	= theirs

Notice

We don't use *its* as a possessive pronoun.

A Change the sentences as in the example.

1. That's my newspaper. → That's mine.

2. It's her car. → _____

3. These are your glasses. → _____

4. Are those their photos? → _____

5. Your hair looks terrible. → _____

6. That dog looks like our dog. → _____

7. I prefer our house to their house. → _____

Learn & Practice 4

Questions with *Whose*

- We use *whose* to ask who something belongs to. *Whose* can be used with or without a noun.

Q: **Whose** hocky stick is that?
A: It is **his** hocky stick.
Q: **Whose** is that hocky stick?
A: It is **his**.

Questions	Answers with Possessives
Whose dog is this? **Whose** is this?	It's **Julia's** dog. It's **her** dog. It's **hers**.
Whose books are those? **Whose** are those?	They're **Kevin's** books. They're **his** books. They're **his**.

Notice

＊Do not confuse *who's* and *whose*.
who's = who is / whose = who owns something

A Write *whose* and choose the correct words.

1. Q: _Whose_ jackets (is / (are)) those?   A: They're (he / his) jackets.

2. Q: _____ bicycle (is / are) that?   A: It is (her / hers).

3. Q: _____ sneakers (is / are) these?   A: They're (Olivia / Olivia's) sneakers.

4. Q: _____ (is / are) those?   A: They're (mine / my).

5. Q: _____ (is / are) that?   A: It's (their / theirs).

A Write descriptions of the things in the pictures. Use *boy*, *girl*, *children*, and these words: *ice skates*, *dog*, *tennis racquet*, *bicycle*, and *skateboards*.

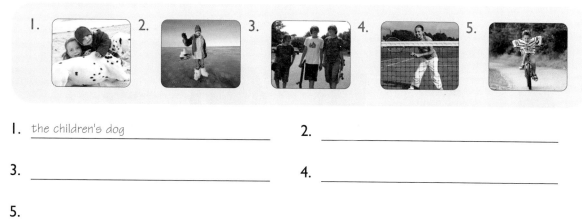

1. the children's dog _____

2. _____

3. _____

4. _____

5. _____

B Make questions with *whose*, *that (those)* and answer them.

bicycle / Jane

T-shirt / Ted

car / my parents

shoes / William

skateboard / Kelly

binoculars / Linda

1. Whose bicycle is that? _____

   It's Jane's. _____

2. _____
   _____

3. _____
   _____

4. _____
   _____

5. _____
   _____

6. _____
   _____

C Look at the pictures of Bob and Jane's room, and use the words in the box to make sentences with *his*, *hers*, or *theirs*. Use a dictionary if necessary.

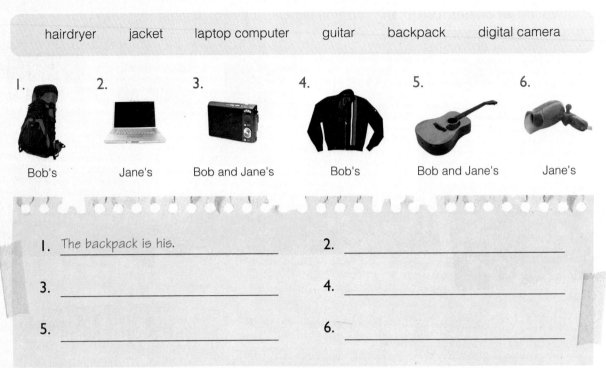

| hairdryer | jacket | laptop computer | guitar | backpack | digital camera |

1. Backpack — Bob's
2. laptop computer — Jane's
3. digital camera — Bob and Jane's
4. jacket — Bob's
5. guitar — Bob and Jane's
6. hairdryer — Jane's

1. The backpack is his.

2. _____

3. _____

4. _____

5. _____

6. _____

D Write sentences using the possessive forms as in the example.

books / teacher   thermometer / nurse   tools / doctor   wrench / mechanic

1. Those are the teacher's books.
   Those are his books. Those are his.

2. _____
   _____

3. _____
   _____

4. _____
   _____

A Look at the example and practice with a partner. (Repeat 3 times.)

I.

 Whose flowers are these?

 They're Erika's flowers.

I.
flowers / Erika

2.
ballpoint pens / Matt

3.
books / Nicole

4.

 Is this your pink dress?

 No, it isn't.

 Whose is this?

 It's Alice's pink dress.

4.
pink dress / Alice

5.
sandwich / Eric

6.
magazine / Anthony

B The teacher touches or points to something in the classroom that belongs to someone and says, "Whose book is this?" A student points to the owner and says, "This is Michelle's . . ."

Whose book is this?

This is Michelle's book.

No, that's Kevin's book.
OR Right. It's my book. / It's mine.
/ Mine.

C Work in pairs. Mix up your belongings. Then sort them out.

This is my pencil.

Yes, and these are your pencils.

Possessives **57**

A Ask and answer, as in the example.

1. Patty / tidy / her room / now? → Yes

   Q: _Is Patty tidying her room now?_   A: _Yes, she is._

2. your brother / work / on his computer / now? → No / have lunch

   Q: _____   A: _____

3. you / do / your homework / at the moment? → Yes

   Q: _____   A: _____

4. Jane / sleep / in the living room? → No / watch TV

   Q: _____   A: _____

B Write the nouns in the plural form.

1. man and woman   _____ dance for rain.

2. foot   Their _____ stomp and swing.

3. sky   The _____ turn cloudy after the dance.

4. raindrop   _____ fall on the cities.

5. child   The _____ find a beautiful rainbow.

C Complete the sentences. Use I/me/you/she/her, etc.

1. I want to see her, but ____she____ doesn't want to see ____me____.

2. We want to see them, but _____ don't want to see _____.

3. She wants to see him, but _____ doesn't want to see _____.

4. You want to see me, but _____ don't want to see _____.

5. They want to see her, but _____ doesn't want to see _____.

D Make questions with *whose*, *this (these)* and answer them.

1.

violin / Rebecca

Q: Whose violin is this?

A: It's Rebecca's violin.

2.

ball / the children

Q: _____

A: _____

3.

shoes / Michael

Q: _____

A: _____

4.

MP3 player / Chloe

Q: _____

A: _____

E Answer the questions. Use the present progressive.

1.

What is Peter doing this Saturday?

→ He is reading a book. _____ (read a book)

2.

What are Ava and Steve doing this Saturday?

→ _____ (see a movie)

3.

What is Jessica doing this Saturday?

→ _____ (play basketball / with her friends)

4.

What are your parents doing this Saturday?

→ _____ (play tennis)

Unit 9 — Count/Noncount Nouns, Quantity Questions

- Answer the questions.
1. How much milk do they have?
2. How much milk does the woman drink?
3. Tell sentences about what there is and what there isn't in your fridge. Use *some* and *any*.

Unit Focus

▶ Count/Noncount Nouns
▶ Units of Measure with Nouns
▶ *A(n), Some, Any*
▶ Quantity Questions

Yes, there is some coffee, but we haven't got any sugar.

Have we got any coffee?

Well, there are two bottles of milk and there is an apple.

OK. Are there any milk or apples in the fridge?

I drink three glasses of milk in a day.

How much milk do you drink?

Learn & Practice 1

Count (or Countble) and Noncount (or Uncountable) Nouns

- We can count some things like books. *Book* is a count (or countable) noun and it can have singular or plural forms.

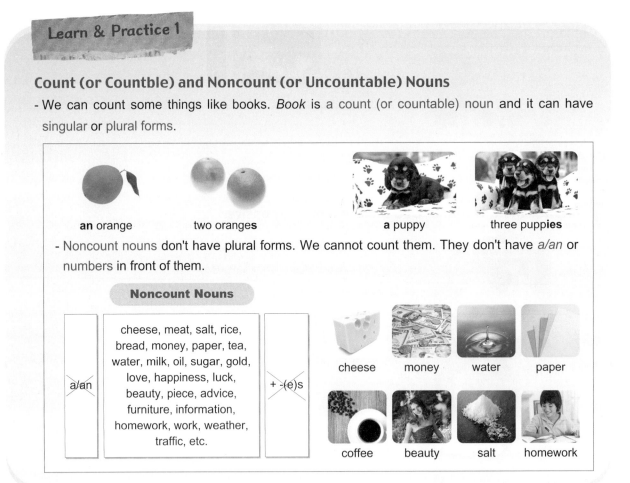

an orange   two orange**s**   **a** puppy   three pupp**ies**

- Noncount nouns don't have plural forms. We cannot count them. They don't have *a/an* or numbers in front of them.

Noncount Nouns

| a/an | cheese, meat, salt, rice, bread, money, paper, tea, water, milk, oil, sugar, gold, love, happiness, luck, beauty, piece, advice, furniture, information, homework, work, weather, traffic, etc. | + -(e)s |

cheese   money   water   paper
coffee   beauty   salt   homework

A Circle the noncount nouns.

1. teacher / (milk)

2. advice / letter

3. chair / furniture

4. lemon / snow

5. sandwich / butter

6. tea / banana

Units of Measure with Nouns

- We use units of measure such as *a cup of coffee* or *a botle of water* to express quantities of noncount nouns.

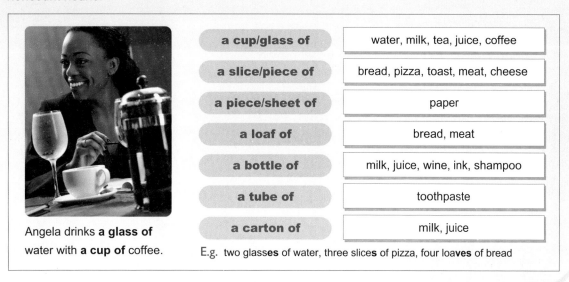

a cup/glass of	water, milk, tea, juice, coffee
a slice/piece of	bread, pizza, toast, meat, cheese
a piece/sheet of	paper
a loaf of	bread, meat
a bottle of	milk, juice, wine, ink, shampoo
a tube of	toothpaste
a carton of	milk, juice

Angela drinks **a glass of** water with **a cup of** coffee.

E.g. two glass**es** of water, three slic**es** of pizza, four loa**ves** of bread

---

(A) Choose and fill in the blanks.

| three pieces of | a bottle of | a carton of | three loaves of |

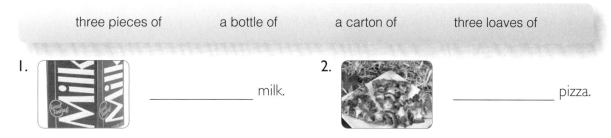

1. _____ milk.

2. _____ pizza.

A(n), *Some*, and *Any*

- We can use *a/an* in front of singular count nouns. Remember that *a* and *an* mean one.
- We use *some/any* to say the amount when we don't know exactly how much or how many.
- We use *some/any* for both count and noncount nouns.

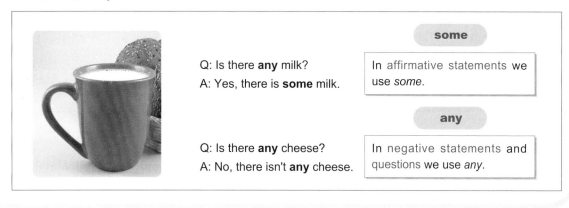

Q: Is there **any** milk?
A: Yes, there is **some** milk.

some

In affirmative statements we use *some*.

Q: Is there **any** cheese?
A: No, there isn't **any** cheese.

any

In negative statements and questions we use *any*.

A Write *a(n)*, *some*, or *any*.

1. There aren't ___any___ eggs in the fridge.

2. I'd like _____ orange juice, please.

3. There is _____ car in the street.

4. I don't have _____ money.

5. I need _____ information about the bus schedule.

6. Are there _____ pictures on the wall?

Learn & Practice 4

Quantity Questions

- In questions, we use *how many* with countable nouns and *how much* with uncountable nouns.
- We use *how much* to ask about the amount of something.
- We use *how many* to ask about the number of things.

Q: **How many** slices of bread do you eat for breakfast?
A: About three.

Q: **How much** milk do you drink every morning?
A: Not much. About two glasses.

A Underline and correct the mistakes.

1. How <u>many</u> sugar is there in your coffee? → ____much____

2. How much meals do you eat every day? → _____

3. How many coffee would you like? → _____

4. How much slices of pizza can you eat? → _____

5. How much hours do you study every day? → _____

6. How many money does a bus ticket cost? → _____

A Complete the dialog with *any* or *some*.

Doctor: Do you eat ___any___ bread?

Kathy: No, I don't eat _____ bread.

Doctor: It's necessary to eat _____ fruit.
Do you drink _____ orange juice at breakfast?

Kathy: Yes, I drink some.

Doctor: You have to drink _____ water after every meal, too.

Kathy: Do I have to eat _____ vegetables?

Doctor: Yes, you have to eat a lot of vegetables.
Do you eat _____ fish?

Kathy: No, I don't eat _____ fish.

B What do you have for breakfast every morning? Use the words in the box to make sentences.

jam   coffee   green tea   muffin   water   cereal   butter   biscuits

cereal

muffin

E.g. Ava has some green tea with a glass of water. She doesn't have any coffee. She has milk with some bread. She also has toast with butter and orange jam. Sometimes she has biscuits with strawberry juice and muffin.

I have _____

_____

_____

_____

C Read the text and write questions with *how much* or *how many* using the words given. Then answer them.

Scott is always hungry. He drinks six glasses of milk. He eats five eggs and seven slices of bread with a lot of butter and cheese. Then he drinks two cups of coffee with four doughnuts. He spends a lot of money on breakfast.

1. Q: _How much milk does he drink?_   A: _He drinks six glasses of milk._
   (milk / drink)

2. Q: _____   A: _____
   (egg / eat)

3. Q: _____   A: _____
   (slices of bread / eat)

4. Q: _____   A: _____
   (doughnuts / have)

5. Q: _____   A: _____
   (coffee / drink)

D Find five noncount nouns and two count nouns related to food in the text in Exercise C.

Noncount Nouns	Count Nouns
1. _____	6. _____
2. _____	7. _____
3. _____	
4. _____	
5. _____	

A Look at the example and practice with a partner. Use the words below or invent your own. (Repeat 3 times.)

1.

 How many different vegetables have you eaten today?

 I have two - beets and parsley.

1. vegetables / beets, parsley	2. fruits / mango, kiwi (= kiwi fruit)	3. drinks / strawberry juice, milk

4.

 Are there any oranges in the fridge?

 No, there aren't any oranges but there are some tomatoes.

4. oranges (x) in the fridge / tomatoes (o)	5. bananas (x) on the table / yogurt (o)	6. ice cream (x) in the fridge / fruits (o)

B Work in a small group. Tell your partners what you usually have for breakfast.

a cup of tea / sugar   yogurt / fruit   bread / jam

two slices of toast   fruit juice   dried seaweed rolls

bacon / eggs   cereal / milk   sandwich / salad

I usually have a sandwich and some bread with a glass of milk for breakfast. I also have some yogurt. Now your turn!

Count/Noncount Nouns, Quantity Questions 65

Will, Articles (Definite/Zero)

- Answer the questions.
1. What will the environment be like in the future?
2. What will our cities be like in the future?
3. What will life be like in the future?

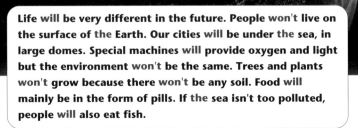

Life will be very different in the future. People won't live on the surface of the Earth. Our cities will be under the sea, in large domes. Special machines will provide oxygen and light but the environment won't be the same. Trees and plants won't grow because there won't be any soil. Food will mainly be in the form of pills. If the sea isn't too polluted, people will also eat fish.

Unit Focus

▶ Will
▶ Definite Article: The

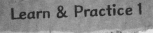

Will

- We use *will* + base verb for the future to make predictions about what we think will happen.
- We also use *will* + base verb for the future when we decide to do something at the time of speaking.

Future Prediction

One day, we **will** go on holiday to the moon.

Decision at the Time of Speaking

Do I look good in this dress?
I **will** buy it.

Future Tense

Affirmative: Will		**Negative: Will Not (= Won't)**	
I/You/We/They He/She/It	**will go** camping tomorrow.	I/You/We/They He/She/It	**won't go** camping tomorrow.

- We can shorten *will* and *will* + *not* with subject pronouns.

I will → I'll   You → You'll   He will → He'll   She will → She'll   They will → They'll   It → It'll

---

Ⓐ Circle the correct words.

1. It will (rain / rains) tomorrow.

2. I will (am / be) a good scientist.

3. They will (gets / get) on a bus.

4. He will (visit / visits) the zoo tomorrow.

B Make sentences in the future tense using *will* or *will not*.

1. I study hard.   →   I will study hard.

2. She doesn't come to the party.   → _____

3. They are not late.   → _____ tomorrow.

4. My mom cooks chicken for dinner. → _____ tonight.

5. Bob is a famous chemist.   → _____ in the future.

Learn & Practice 2

Will: *Yes/No* Questions

- We put *will* at the beginning of the sentence to make a question.

Q: **Will** you arrive at 10:00 tomorrow?
A: Yes, I **will**. / No, I **won't**.

Q: **Will** Olivia watch a movie tonight?
A: No, she **won't**. She **will** listen to music.

Questions	Answers
Will you study tomorrow?	Yes, I **will**. / No, I **won't**.
Will she go camping?	Yes, she **will**. / No, she **won't**.
Will he go fishing?	Yes, he **will**. / No, he **won't**.
Will they buy the car?	Yes, they **will**. / No, they **won't**.
Will it be cold tomorrow?	Yes, it **will**. / No, it **won't**.

- Do not use contractions in affirmative short answers. E.g. Yes, they will. (O) / Yes, ~~they'll~~. (X)

A Make *yes/no* questions and answer them.

1. She will become a figure skater.   Q: Will she become a figure skater?   A: No, she won't .

2. It will be sunny tomorrow.   Q: _____   A: Yes, _____ .

3. He will get married next year.   Q: _____   A: No, _____ .

4. People will live in space colonies. Q: _____   A: Yes, _____ .

Definite Article: *The*

- We use *the* to talk about something specific.
- We use *the* when the person we are speaking to knows which person or thing we are talking about.

I can see **a** hat. **The** hat is brown.
(Which hat? The specific hat in the picture. The noun is mentioned for a second time or is already known.)

Bob: Where's Jeff?
Peter: He's in **the** house.
(Both Bob and Peter know which house they are talking about.)

- *The* is used for only one thing or musical instruments.

the Earth   **the** Moon   Lisa is playing **the** piano.   He can play **the** drums.

- We don't use any articles before subjects, sports, languages, meals, cities, and counties.

Q: Do you like **baseball**?
A: No, I like **soccer**.

Subjects: history, science, math
Sports: soccer, basketball, baseball
Languages: English, Korean, Japanese
Meals: breakfast, lunch, dinner
Cities: Seoul, London, Seattle
Countries: France, Korea, China

Ⓐ Write *a(n)*, *the*, or X (if you don't need an article) to complete the sentences.

1. Look at ___the___ sky.

2. I like _____ soccer.

3. Where are _____ children?

4. _____ London is a big city.

5. Where's Tom? He is in _____ kitchen.

6. It's time for _____ lunch now!

7. _____ sun is a star.

8. My sister lives in _____ Singapore.

A What will Laila do tomorrow? Make sentences with *will* or *won't*.

1. ☐O☐ drive an electric car

2. ☐X☐ go to the supermarket

3. ☐O☐ help Susan move from her apartment

4. ☐X☐ take the dog for a walk

5. ☐O☐ finish her project

1. Laila will drive an electric car tomorrow.

2. _____

3. _____

4. _____

5. _____

B Use the prompts to write sentences with *will*. Use short forms where possible.

1. It's 9:00. Mary is still in bed. (miss / the school bus)

   → She'll miss the school bus.

2. Lucifer's new book sells very well. (become / a best-seller)

   → _____

3. Steve is exhausted. There are still 20 km to run. (not / finish / the race)

   → _____

4. They are the home team. The score is 4-0. There are ten minutes left. (win / the game)

   → _____

5. It is 10:00. My plane leaves 10:10. I'm 30 km from the airport. (not / catch / my plane)

   → _____

6. It's very cloudy today. We can see big black clouds and lightning. (be / a thunderstorm)

   → _____

C Fill in the blanks with *a*, *an*, or *the*. Put an **X** if you don't need an article.

1. "Where's Bob?" "He's in ___the___ kitchen."

2. She's _____ good musician: she plays _____ flute beautifully.

3. It's _____ nice morning. Let's go for _____ walk.

4. *Orders* is _____ bookstore. _____ shop next to it is _____ famous bakery.

5. We had _____ dinner at a restaurant last night.

6. Neil Armstrong was _____ astronaut. He was _____ first man to walk on _____ moon.

D Look at the pictures. Make questions and answer them.

1.

they / go to the movies (x)
→ paint the house (o)

2.

all the family / be at the wedding (x)
→ at the park (o)

3.

Chris / wash his clothes (x)
→ play the violin (o)

4.

Linda / hang out with her friends (x)
→ go shopping with her mom (o)

1. Q: Will they go to the movies?
   A: No, they won't. They will paint the house.

2. Q: _____
   A: No, they won't. _____

3. Q: _____
   A: No, he won't. _____

4. Q: _____
   A: No, she won't. _____

A Look at the example and practice with a partner. Use the words below or invent your own. (Repeat 3 times.)

I.

 They won't watch TV.

 They will have dinner.

I.

they / watch TV (x)
→ have dinner (o)

2.

Jack / read a newspaper (x)
→ clean his room (o)

3.

they / go on a picnic tomorrow (x)
→ go fishing tomorrow (o)

4.

 Will you go to the zoo tomorrow?   No, I won't.

 Where will you go?   I will go to the museum tomorrow.

4.

you / zoo (x) → museum (o)

5.

Kathy / bank (x) → gym (o)

6.

they / theater (x) → bakery (o)

B Interview! Talk about the questions below with a partner and write.

1. Will there be a cure for cancer in 10 years?

2. What do you think the future will be like?

3. Do you think there will be as many cars as today?

4. Will people live on Mars one day?

5. Will robots do all the work at home?

6. In the future, what do you think schools will be like?

My partner: _____ (name)

I. Yes, _____.
   No, _____.

2. I think _____.

3. Yes, I think _____.
   No, I think _____.

4. Yes, _____.
   No, _____.

5. Yes, _____.
   No, _____.

6. In my opinion, schools will _____
   _____.

Simple Past of *Be*

• Answer the questions.
1. Do you know who King Sejong is?
2. Do you know who invented Hangeul?
3. Why do most Koreans today think Hangeul is the best writing system in the world?

Unit Focus

► Affirmatives
► Negatives
► Questions

Sejong was born in 1397. Sejong was the 3rd son of King, Taejong. He was the 4th king of Joseon. Sejong was a great king. He invented Hangeul (the Korean Alphabet) in 1443. It was very easy, so everyone could learn and write it. Hangeul is a very scientific writing system. Hangeul has 10 vowels and 14 consonants. Now it is UNESCO World Heritage.

Learn & Practice 1

Simple Past: *Be*

- We use the simple past for actions which began and ended in the past, or to describe situations in the past. For this reason, we often use the verb with time expressions like *yesterday, two hours ago, last week, in 1999.*

- The simple past of the verb *be* has two forms: *was* and *were*.

Past	Now

Brandon **was** a student 10 years ago. He **was** 20 years old.	Brandon **is** an English teacher now. He **is** 30 years old.

Subject	Be
I/he/she/it	was
you/we/they	were

A Complete the sentences using *was* or *were*.

1. It ___was___ cold yesterday.

2. We _____ in New York in 1999.

3. I _____ tired yesterday.

4. Tom and Ben _____ at the party last night.

5. You _____ late yesterday.

6. They _____ very happy together.

Past of *Be*: Negatives

- To make a negative statement, we put *not* after *be*: was not / were not

| I **wasn't** a lawyer. I **was** a doctor. | He **wasn't** at the park. He **was** at home. | We **weren't** teachers. We **were** students. | They **weren't** happy. They **were** sad. |

Negative

Pronouns	Be	Not		Contractions
I	was			I **wasn't**
you	were	not	➡	you **weren't**
he/she/it	was			he/she/it **wasn't**
we/they	were			we/they **weren't**

- We usually use contractions when we speak: *wasn't / weren't*

A Look at the pictures and fill in the blanks with *wasn't* or *weren't*.

1.

They ___weren't___ at the bus stop.

2.

William _____ a prosecutor.

3.

Jane and Tom _____ happy yesterday.

4.

Leonardo da Vinci _____ American.

5.

She _____ a ballerina.

6.

Mozart _____ an actor.

Past of *Be*: *Yes/No* Questions

- To make a question, we put *was/were* before the subject. *Yes/No* questions end with a question mark (?).

Q: **Was** Michelangelo a painter?
A: Yes, he was.
Q: **Was** he German?
A: No, he wasn't. He was an Italian.

Questions	Answers	
Was I . . .?	Yes, you **were**.	No, you **weren't**.
Were you . . .?	Yes, I **was**.	No, I **wasn't**.
Was he/she/it . . .?	Yes, he/she/it **was**.	No, he/she/it **wasn't**.
Were we . . .?	Yes, you **were**.	No, you **weren't**.
Were you . . .?	Yes, we **were**.	No, we **weren't**.
Were they . . .?	Yes, they **were**.	No, they **weren't**.

(A) Complete *yes/no* questions and answer them.

1. ___Was___ it sunny yesterday?

Yes, _____.   No, _____.

2. _____ you a speed skater?

Yes, _____.   No, _____.

3. _____ she a tennis player?

Yes, _____.   No, _____.

A Use the prompts below to ask and answer questions, as in the example.

1.

Nadia Comaneci / artist?
→ No / gymnast

1. Q: Was Nadia Comaneci an artist?
   A: No, she wasn't. She was a gymnast.

2.

Neil Armstrong / professor?
→ No / astronaut

2. Q: _____
   A: _____
   _____

3. Q: _____
   A: _____
   _____

3.

Thomas Edison / president?
→ No / inventor

B Look at the pictures and write correct sentences about the people.

Ten Years Ago . . .

1.
2.
3.
4.

Destiny: singer (X)
fashion model (O)

Bob: painter (X)
doctor (O)

Sandra: fat (X)
slender (O)

Sujin and Minho: teachers (X)
students (O)

1. Destiny wasn't a singer. She was a fashion model.

2. _____

3. _____

4. _____

C Look at the pictures and write questions and answers. Use a dictionary if necessary.

| restaurant | train station | supermarket | movie theater |

1.

Peter / last Tuesday?

Q: Where _____was Peter last Tuesday_____ ?

A: _He was at the supermarket._

2.

you and your friends / last Saturday?

Q: Where _____

_____ ?

A: _____

3.

Emma and her parents / yesterday afternoon?

Q: Where _____

_____ ?

A: _____

4.

Jessica / last night?

Q: Where _____ ?

A: _____

D Put in *wasn't* or *weren't* and the words from the box. Make sure you understand actually. Use a dictionary if necessary.

| interesting | in England | a teacher | late | with Alex |

1. You _____weren't late_____ . Actually you arrived 5 minutes early.

2. The lesson _____ . Actually it was very boring.

3. I wasn't _____ . Actually I was with Ava.

4. We _____ last week. We went to Singapore for a few days.

5. My mother _____ . Actually, she worked as a taxi driver.

A Look at the example and practice with a partner. Use the words below or invent your own. (Repeat 3 times.)

1.

 Where was Philip at seven o'clock yesterday evening?

 He was at the art gallery.

1. Philip / at seven o'clock yesterday evening?
→ at the art gallery

2. Sophie / at twenty past twelve?
→ at the shopping center

3. Toni and Marvin / at half past ten last night?
→ in the movie theater

4.

 When I was young, I was a good singer.

 When she was young, she was a fashion designer.

4. I good singer — she fashion designer

5. I call center worker — he football player

6. I very intelligent — they explorers

B Ask your partner questions with *Wh- were you . . .?* Use the ideas below or invent your own.

- what / favorite toy / when young
- who / favorite teacher at school
- who / best friend(s) / when ten years old
- where / last weekend
- where / at 9 o'clock last night
- what / favorite food / three years ago
- how old / in 2003

Where were you at 9 o'clock last night?

I was at home.

My partner: _____ (name)

When he (or she) was young, his (or her) favorite toy was a teddy bear. His (or Her) favorite teacher at school was _____

_____

Simple Past of *Be* 77

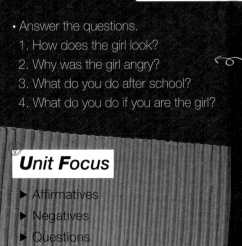

• Answer the questions.
1. How does the girl look?
2. Why was the girl angry?
3. What do you do after school?
4. What do you do if you are the girl?

Unit Focus

► Affirmatives
► Negatives
► Questions

Friday, May 10

After school I finished my homework quickly. I didn't want to stay at home, so I called Peter and we decided to watch Harry Potter. The movie started at four o'clock p.m. I waited for him for one hour but he didn't come. So I walked home without seeing the movie, and today I feel terrible!

Learn & Practice 1

Simple Past: Regular Verbs

- We use the simple past to talk about actions and situations that began and ended in the past.
- To form the simple past of regular verbs, we add -ed to the base form of the verb.
- To make the negative of the simple past, we add did not before base verbs.

Lucy **worked** in a hospital last year.
She **helped** a lot of people.

They **didn't play** soccer yesterday.
They **played** basketball.

Affirmative	
I/We/You He/She/It/They	worked.

Negative	
I/We/You He/She/It/They	didn't work.

* subject + did not (= didn't) + base verb

Ⓐ **Write the verbs in the past tense.**

1. We _____watched_____ (watch) TV yesterday.

2. You _____ (not answer) the phone.

3. It _____ (rain) last night.

4. Three years ago, Tiffany _____ (work) at a bakery.

5. They _____ (not visit) my house last year.

Simple Past: *Yes/No* Questions

- To make a *yes/no question*, we put *did* at the beginning of the sentence. We always use the base verb after the subject.
- We often use *did* in short answers to questions.

Q: Did Olivia talk to Tom yesterday?
A: No, she didn't. She talked to Steve.

Did	Subject	Base Verb
Did	I/We/You He/She/It/They	work?

Answers	
Yes, I (we, he . . .) **did**.	**No**, I (we, he . . .) **didn't**.

Ⓐ Write the sentences in the question form.

1. They played baseball yesterday. → *Did they play baseball yesterday?*

2. We watched the movie last Saturday. → _____

3. She moved to Singapore. → _____

4. It rained yesterday. → _____

5. He walked downtown yesterday. → _____

Ⓑ Look at the pictures and answer the questions.

1.  Did he wash his hair?
→ *No, he didn't.*

2.  Did it snow yesterday?
→ _____

3.  Did you paint a picture last night?
→ _____

4.  Did Alicia walk to school yesterday?
→ _____

Spelling of Regular Past Verbs

- To form the affirmative past tense of most regular verbs:

answer → answer**ed**	walk → walk**ed**	• Add **-ed** to most verbs.	
help → help**ed**	paint → paint**ed**		
visit → visit**ed**	listen → listen**ed**		
arrive → arriv**ed**	hope → hop**ed**	• If a verb ends in **-e**, add **-d**.	
invite → invit**ed**	like → lik**ed**		
study → stud**ied**	cry → cr**ied**	• If a verb ends in **a consonant + -y**, change the **-y** to **-i** before the **-ed**.	
try → tr**ied**	carry → carr**ied**		
stop → stop**ped**	plan → plan**ned**	• If a verb ends in **a vowel + a consonant**, **double the consonant** before the **-ed**.	
prefer → prefer**red**			

A Write the simple past of these verbs.

1. stay → _stayed_

2. listen → _____

3. study → _____

4. love → _____

5. cry → _____

6. work → _____

7. carry → _____

8. wash → _____

9. start → _____

10. want → _____

11. stop → _____

12. live → _____

13. plan → _____

14. try → _____

15. invite → _____

B Complete the sentences in the past tense.

1. | invite | I ___invited___ all my friends to my birthday party last year.

2. | study | Olivia _____ Japanese last night.

3. | play | She _____ the piano yesterday.

4. | walk | He _____ to the bus stop.

5. | arrive | Tina was very tired when she _____ home.

6. | plan | They _____ a family outing with me.

A Look at the chart and write sentences about what William did and didn't do yesterday, as in the example.

	✓	X
1. clean	the garage	bedroom
2. visit	uncle	grandparents
3. study	Korean	Japanese
4. watch	a movie	the news
5. listen to	music on the radio	English CDs

1. Yesterday William cleaned the garage, but he didn't clean his bedroom.

2. _____

_____

3. _____

_____

4. _____

_____

5. _____

_____

B Choose and write about you.

clean my room	play in the park	study for the test	visit my aunt
cook dinner	brush my teeth	listen to music	watch a DVD
study English	watch a movie	walk to school	help my mother/father

Things I Did Yesterday

1. I played in the park yesterday.

3. _____

5. _____

7. _____

Things I Didn't Do Yesterday

2. I didn't watch a DVD yesterday.

4. _____

6. _____

8. _____

C Look at the pictures and the prompts. Write questions and answers as in the example.

1.

Amy / talk to / Tom / yesterday?
→ No / talk to / Steve

Did Amy talk to Tom
yesterday?

No, she didn't. She talked to
Steve.

2.

the boy / clean / the house / last
Friday? → No / wash / the car

_____

_____

_____

_____

3.

Kelly / visit / her friends / last night?
→ No / stay / at home

_____

_____

_____

_____

D Find and write about these people.

☐ the Nobel Peace Prize
   in 1979

☐ Guernica in 1937

☐ the oceans

☐ the 9th symphony in
   1822-1824

☐ in space

☐ Mickey Mouse

☐ penicillin

☐ the telephone

☐ the soldiers

1. **Beethoven**

compose

4. **Florence Nightingale**

help

7. **Pablo Picasso**

paint

2. **Mother Teresa**

receive

5. **Alexander Bell**

invent

8. **Valentina Tereshkova**

travel

3. **Alexander Fleming**

discover

6. **Jacques Cousteau**

explore

9. **Walt Disney**

create

1. Beethoven composed the 9th symphony in 1822-1824.

2. _____

3. _____

4. _____

5. _____

6. _____

7. _____

8. _____

9. _____

A Look at the example and practice with a partner. Use the words below or invent your own. (Repeat 3 times.)

I.

 Did Nick visit Buckingham Palace last year?

 No, he didn't. He visited Trafalgar Square.

I.

Nick

visit / Buckingham Palace / last year?
→ No / visit Trafalgar Square

2.

Linda

go camping / yesterday?
→ No / stay at home

3.

Paul

clean / his room / last night?
→ No / play computer games

B Work in pairs. Choose five of the activities in the vocabulary box to complete the table below. Don't tell your partner. Ask your partner questions, as in the example.

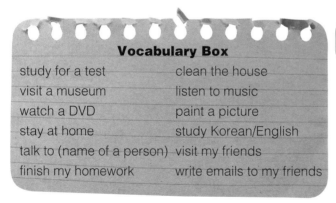

Vocabulary Box

study for a test	clean the house
visit a museum	listen to music
watch a DVD	paint a picture
stay at home	study Korean/English
talk to (name of a person)	visit my friends
finish my homework	write emails to my friends

I played soccer yesterday. Did you play soccer yesterday?

Yes, I did. OR No, I didn't.

	You	Your Partner
yesterday		
two days ago		
last night/Saturday, etc.		
three hours ago		
last week		

Unit 13 Simple Past 2

• Answer the questions.

1. Who went to the party with her brother?
2. Who went home on foot?
3. What did you do last night?

Unit Focus

▶ Irregular Verbs
▶ WH- Questions with Action Verbs

Ava   Olivia

Olivia: Did you go out last night, Ava?
Ava: Yes, I went to the party with my brother. We had a great time!
Olivia: How did you get home?
Ava: We caught the last bus. Another girl, however, wasn't very lucky.
        She ran after the bus, but she missed it! It was very funny!
Olivia: That was me! I didn't find it funny!

Learn & Practice 1

Simple Past: Irregular Verbs

- Some verbs do not have -ed forms. They each have different changes.
- To form negatives, questions, and short answers in the simple past, we use *did/didn't* and the base form of the main verb.

I **got up** at seven o'clock yesterday morning.

Nancy and I **went** to a haunted house last night.
We **met** a ghost there.

- The following are some of the most common irregular verbs.

Base Form	Past Form	Base Form	Past Form
buy	**bought**	come	**came**
see	**saw**	make	**made**
take	**took**	eat	**ate**
drink	**drank**	sit	**sat**
feel	**felt**	get	**got**
give	**gave**	go	**went**
have	**had**	hear	**heard**
write	**wrote**	read	**read**
sleep	**slept**	meet	**met**
find	**found**	put	**put**
fly	**flew**	speak	**spoke**

A Complete the table. Use the simple present or the simple past.

Base Form		Past Form	Base Form		Past Form
buy	→	bought	come	→	
	→	saw		→	made
take	→		eat	→	
drink	→			→	sat
	→	felt	get	→	
give	→		go	→	
	→	had		→	heard
write	→		read	→	
sleep	→		meet	→	
	→	found		→	put
fly	→		speak	→	

B Change the sentences to the past tense.

1.
   Mark speaks on his phone.
   → Mark spoke on his phone. _____

2.
   Christina buys some flowers.
   → _____

3.
   Kelly and Betty eat lunch at the cafeteria.
   → _____

4.
   Tiffany goes to bed early.
   → _____

5.
   I write a letter to my parents.
   → _____

Simple Past: *WH-* Questions with Action Verbs

- *WH-* questions with action verbs in the past use *did* as the helping verb.
- An information question begins with a question word.

Sunny: **Where did** you **go** on Saturday?
Lisa: I went to the beach.
Sunny: **What did** you **do**?
Lisa: I went surfing, of course.

WH- Word	Did	Subject	Base Verb
Where		you	**go** yesterday?
What		I	**talk** about?
When		we	**go** to the beach?
What time	did	you	**get** there?
Who		he	**call**?
How		she	**know** the secret?
Why		they	**run**?

WH- Word as Subject	Past Tense Verb
Who	**rang** you?
What	**happened**?

- When *who* and *what* are the subject of a sentence, we do not need the auxiliary verb. For instance, in the sentence *who did you meet?*, the subject is *you* so it is necessary. But in *Who came yesterday?* the subject is *who* so we do not need the auxiliary verb.

Ⓐ Choose and write the questions to complete the dialogs.

> Why did you stay home?   When did you come to this city?   Where did you go yesterday?

1.

A: *Where did you go yesterday?*
_____
B: I went to the zoo.

2.

A: _____
_____
B: Because I was tired.

3.

A: _____
_____
B: I came to this city two weeks ago.

A Look at the pictures. Use the phrases in the simple past to write what the people did yesterday.

drink green tea   go to the movie theater   ride his bicycle   eat cherries   catch the bus

1.

Michelle usually watches TV on Sundays, but yesterday she
went to the movie theater .

2.

Steve usually goes to school by car, but yesterday he
_____ .

3.

They usually have cake for dessert, but yesterday they
_____ .

4.

David usually plays soccer on Saturdays, but yesterday he
_____ .

5.

Anthony usually drinks coffee in the morning, but yesterday he
_____ .

B Complete the paragraph about Joe's holiday. Use the simple past of the verbs in the box.

feed   swim   have   stay   help   wake   take   do

talk   go (x2)

I love summer vacation. Last summer my brother and I _went_ to a village. We _____ on our grandparents' farm and we _____ a great holiday. Every morning we _____ up early and _____ our grandparents. We _____ the animals and _____ many other interesting things. In the afternoon we _____ fishing to the river and _____ in the river. In the evening, after dinner, we _____ a walk around the farm and _____ to our grandparents. It was the best experience of my life!

C Look at the pictures and write questions and answers, as in the example.

1.

Who / Lisa / meet at the restaurant?

Q: Who did Lisa meet at the
   restaurant?

A: She met her friends.

2.

Where / Sue / go yesterday?

Q: _____

_____

A: _____

3.

What / Olivia / buy last week?

Q: _____

_____

A: _____

4.

How / Dennis / get to work yesterday?

Q: _____

_____

A: _____

5.

What / Daniel and Tanya / have for lunch?

Q: _____

_____

A: _____

D Write questions for the answers. Use the underlined words to help you choose the correct question words.

1. Q: Where did Amy and her sister go? _____ A: Amy and her sister went to Singapore.

2. Q: _____ A: Sarah came out of hospital this morning.

3. Q: _____ A: The children bought CDs.

4. Q: _____ A: Dave had a bad day yesterday.

5. Q: _____ A: Laura left a bicycle in the garden.

6. Q: _____ A: I saw her in the afternoon.

A Work in pairs. The following people are telling lies. Read what they say, and then use the words in brackets to correct the false statements.

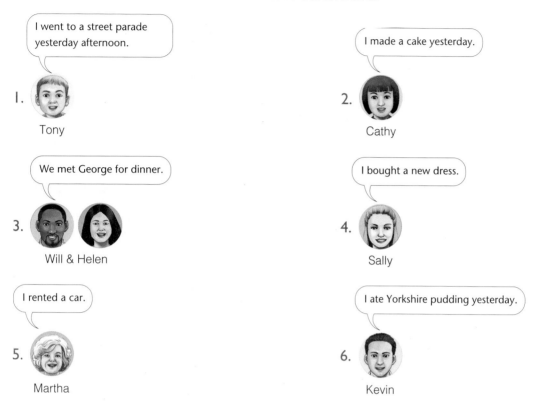

1. Tony — I went to a street parade yesterday afternoon.

2. Cathy — I made a cake yesterday.

3. Will & Helen — We met George for dinner.

4. Sally — I bought a new dress.

5. Martha — I rented a car.

6. Kevin — I ate Yorkshire pudding yesterday.

1.

> Tony went to a street parade yesterday afternoon.
>
> No, he didn't go to a street parade.
> He went to a party yesterday afternoon.

1. No → (party)

2. No → (biscuits)

3. No → (lunch)

4. No → (cardigan)

5. No → (bicycle)

6. No → (roast beef)

A   **Circle the correct words.**

1. Nancy didn't ((enjoy) / enjoyed) the trip to Wales a week ago.

2. Did you (like / liked) the concert?

3. William (goes / went) rollerblading last Saturday.

4. What did you (ate / eat) for lunch?

B   **Fill in *some* or *any*.**

1. Is there _____ pizza?   2. There aren't _____ desks in the classroom.

3. There is _____ milk in the fridge.   4. There aren't _____ towels in the bathroom.

C   **Complete with *how much* or *how many*.**

1. _____ cups of tea do you drink?

2. _____ carrot juice is there in the fridge?

3. _____ chocolate do you eat a week?

4. _____ students are there in your calss?

D   **Put the words in the correct order to make questions.**

1. Alice / at home / yesterday / was   →   _____

2. good / party / was / the   →   _____

3. teacher / mother / your / was / a   →   _____

4. you / a / were / speed skater   →   _____

E   **Look at Jason's agenda for yesterday and make sentences.**

8:00 a.m. walk the dog (O)   2:00 p.m. work on a computer (O)

9:00 a.m. play golf (X)   7:00 p.m. cook dinner (X)

12:00 a.m. cook lunch (O)   9:00 p.m. watch a DVD (X)

1. Yesterday, Jason walked the dog.

2. Yesterday, Jason didn't play golf.

3. _____

4. _____

5. _____

6. _____

F **Match the phrases on the left with the uncountable nouns on the right.**

1. a cup of
2. two loaves of
3. a tube of
4. three slices of
5. a bottle of

- toothpaste
- water
- pizza
- bread
- coffee

G **Look and complete the sentences.**

study hard (O)

listen to music (X)

eat lunch at the cafeteria (O)

do homework (X)

1. Janet ___will study hard___ tomorrow.
   She ___won't listen to music___ tomorrow.

2. They _____
   this Friday.
   They _____
   this Friday.

H **Write the sentences into the simple past form. Then write them in the question form and the negative form.**

1. She gets up early in the morning.
   → She got up early in the morning.
   → Did she get up early in the morning?
   → She didn't get up early in the morning.

2. He teaches history at the university.
   → _____
   → _____
   → _____

3. She writes a letter to her parents.
   → _____
   → _____
   → _____

4. The birds flies away to other countries.
   → _____
   → _____
   → _____

Prepositions of Place

- Answer the questions.
1. Where is your bed?
2. Where is your backpack?
3. Where is your cell phone?
4. Where are your parents now?

ⓘ **Unit Focus**

▶ *In, On, At, Under*
▶ *Behind, Between, Next To*
▶ *In Front Of, Near, Across From,*
  Above, Below

night table

picture

pillows

sofa

bed

This is my bedroom. There is a sofa next to a night table. There is a bed between the night tables. There are pillows on the bed. There is a picture above the bed.

Learn & Practice 1

Prepositions of Place: *In, On, At, Under*

- Prepositions of place **show where something or someone is** located.

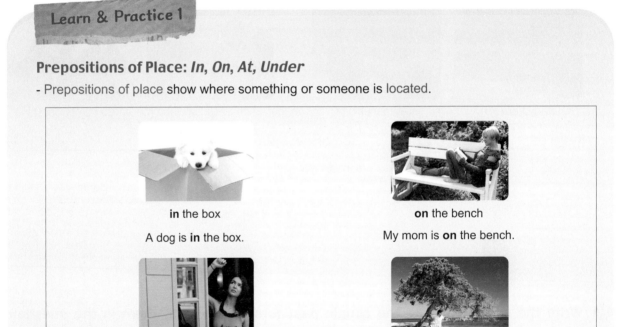

in the box

A dog is **in** the box.

on the bench

My mom is **on** the bench.

at the door

The woman is standing **at** the door.

under the tree

There is a man **under** the tree.

Ⓐ **Look at the picture and circle the correct prepositions.**

1. The clock is (in / on) the wall.

2. The book is (under / on) the table.

3. The basketball is (in / under) the table.

4. The flowers are (in / on) the vase.

Prepositions of Place: *Behind, Between, Next To*

- Prepositions of place show where something or someone is located.

behind the door

My brother is **behind** the door.

Mary   Kathy

between Mary **and** Kathy

I sat **between** Mary **and** Kathy.

next to the window

Bob is **next to** the window.

by the ocean (= **next to** the ocean)

Our house is **by** the ocean.

A Look at the pictures and write the correct prepositions.

1.

Steve is sitting ___*next to / by*___ Lisa.

2.

Kevin   Brian   Scott

Brian is _____ Kevin and Scott.

3.

My daughter is _____ me.

4.

My sister is standing _____ the car.

Prepositions of Place: *In Front Of, Near, Across From, Above, Below*

- Prepositions of place show where something or someone is located.

in front of the Eiffel Tower

A fashion model is standing **in front of** the Eiffel Tower.

near our house

We took a long walk along the ocean **near** our house.

across from the building

The man is **across from** the building.

above the sofa / **below** the picture

The picture is **above** the sofa.
The sofa is **below** the picture.

Ⓐ Look at the pictures and complete the sentences.

1.

The family is standing _____ the bus.

2.

One man is sitting _____ the other man.

3.

The pictures are _____ the bed.

4.

The motor boat is _____ the coast.

A Look at the pictures and complete the sentences.

1.

   sofa

   Q: Where is the boy?

   A: He is _____ behind the sofa _____ .

2.

   box

   Q: Where are the shoes?

   A: They are _____ .

3.

   tree

   Q: Where is the monkey?

   A: It is _____ .

4.

   table

   Q: Where are Brianna and her mother?

   A: They are _____ .

B Look at each picture. Write a sentence using *there is* or *there are* and the idea expressed in the picture and the clue words.

1.

   picture / sofa / above

2.

   laptop / dog / next to

3.

   blanket / baby / under

4.

   girls / boys / across from

1. There is a picture above the sofa.

2. _____
   _____

3. _____
   _____

4. _____
   _____

C Find these things in the picture. Write the numbers.

1. bag _5_   2. glasses ___   3. gloves ___   4. lamp ___   5. pen ___

6. shirt ___   7. socks ___   8. torch ___   9. shoes ___   10. trousers ___

D Look at the picture again. Complete the questions and answers. Use *behind, in, near, on, in front of, under, above,* and *below.*

1. Where _is the pen_ ? ~ _It's on_ the table, _in front of_ the computer.

2. Where _are the gloves_ ? ~ _They're on_ the table, _behind_ the computer.

3. Where _____ ? ~ _____ the floor, _____ the table.

4. Where _____ ? ~ _____ the floor, _____ the chair.

5. Where _____ ? ~ _____ the floor, _____ the chair.

6. Where _____ ? ~ _____ the shelf, _____ the alarm clock.

7. Where _____ ? ~ _____ the shelf, _____ the alarm clock.

8. Where _____ ? ~ _____ the wardrobe, _____ the trousers.

9. Where _____ ? ~ _____ the wardrobe, _____ the socks.

10. Where _____ ? ~ _____ the floor, _____ the wardrobe.

A Look at the example and practice with a partner. Use the words below or invent your own. (Repeat 3 times.)

I.

 Is the girl next to the bench?

 No, she isn't. She is on the bench.

1.

the girl / next to / the bench?
→ No / on

2.

the man / by / the umbrella?
→ No / under

3.

Tom / in front of / the tree?
→ No / behind

4.

Alice / behind / the piano?
→ No / in front of

B Work with a partner. Ask and answer questions about the buildings in your neighborhood.

Is there a supermarket in your neighborhood?

Yes, there is.
It's next to the cafeteria. /
It's across from the post office.

Your turn now.

Prepositions of Time

• Read and answer the questions.

1. What time do you go to school?
2. What is your favorite movie?
3. What do you usually do on the weekend?
4. Do you like rollerblading? Why? Why not?

On the weekend I always have a great time. I get up **at** 8 o'clock **on** Saturday mornings and play badminton with my father. **In** the afternoons I go to the movie theater. Sundays are good, too. I go to the park and I go rollerblading with my friends. **In** the evenings I watch DVDs. Horror movies are my favorite.

Unit Focus

▶ *At, In, On*
▶ Questions with *When, What Day,* and *What Time*

Learn & Practice 1

Prepositions of Time: *At, In, On*

- We use prepositions of time to say when something happens.
- We use *at* before exact times, special holiday periods, and night.

We go to school **at** 7 o'clock.

Koreans enjoy the full moon **at** night on Chuseok.

At
at 2 o'clock
at 11:00 a.m.
at night
at lunchtime

- We use *in* before months, years, seasons, and longer periods of time.

The Korean War broke out **in** 1950.

I usually work **in** the morning.

In
in the morning/evening
in April/May/June, etc.
in (the) summer/winter
in 1999/2002

- We use *on* before days, dates, and when we refer to a particular part of a day.

I'm always sleepy **on** Monday mornings.

I will see you **on** Monday.

On
on Saturdays
on Christmas Day
on Friday morning
on Wednesday
on May 25, 2013
on the weekend

A Write the time prepositions: *at*, *in*, or *on*.

1. We have a class _____ ten o'clock.

2. She studies _____ night.

3. My daughter was born _____ 2008.

4. We first met _____ a cold evening in April.

5. There are no classes _____ Saturday.

6. It is very cold _____ winter.

7. I usually go swimming _____ Tuesdays.

8. How many people are there _____ Korea?

Learn & Practice 2

Questions with *When*, *What Day*, and *What Time*

- We use *when* or *what* for questions about time. When we talk about time, we usually use the prepositions: *at*, *in*, or *on*.

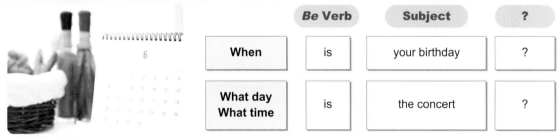

	Be Verb	Subject	?
When	is	your birthday	?
What day **What time**	is	the concert	?

Q: **When** is your birthday?
A: It's **on** June 18th. It's **on** Friday.
Q: **What time** is your birthday party?
A: It's **at** 7:00.

	Helping Verb	Subject	Base Verb
When **What time**	do	I/you/we/they	get up?
	does	he/she/it	

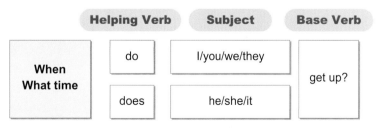

Q: **When** do you clean your room?
A: I clean my room **on** Saturdays.

Q: **What time** do you clean your room?
A: I clean my room **at** 7 o'clock.

A Complete the questions with *when* or *what time*.

1. ___When___ is the play? ~ The play is on Monday.

2. _____ is her class? ~ Her class is on Friday morning.

3. _____ is her class? ~ Her class is at 11:30.

4. _____ is your birthday? ~ It's on May 15th. It's on Friday.

5. _____ do you go shopping? ~ I go shopping at 4 o'clock.

6. _____ do you go shopping? ~ I go shopping on Saturdays.

7. _____ does the bank open? ~ It opens at 8 a.m.

B Unscramble the words to make questions.

1. you / use / do / this camcoder / when → *When do you use this camcoder?*

2. when / the concert / is → _____

3. our flight / when / is → _____

4. do / you / what / get up / time → _____

5. do / time / you / eat / what / dinner → _____

C Read the questions. Then complete the answers with the correct preposition.

1. Q: What time does the bookstore open?
   A: The bookstore opens __at__ 9 a.m.

2. Q: What time do you eat breakfast?
   A: I eat breakfast _____ 7:30 in the morning.

3. Q: What time does he start work?
   A: He starts work at 8:00 _____ the morning.

4. Q: When does she go on vacation?
   A: She goes on vacation _____ summer.

5. Q: When does he clean his apartment?
   A: He cleans his apartment _____ Sundays.

A Complete the blanks with the verbs in brackets and *at*, *in*, *on*, as in the example.

1. Emily and Claire ___do___ (do) their homework ___in___ the afternoon.

2. Michael _____ (clean) his room _____ Saturday morning.

3. My mother _____ (wake) up _____ 6:00 _____ the morning.

4. Justin and his sister Sarah _____ (visit) their grandparents _____ the weekend.

B Complete the text with *in* or *at*.

Patricia gets up ___at___ 7:00 _____ the morning. She has breakfast _____ 7:30 and _____ 8:00 leaves for school. _____ lunchtime, she has lunch at school. She gets home _____ 3:00 _____ the afternoon. She listens to music, then does her homework. She has dinner _____ 7 o'clock and then watches TV. She goes to bed _____ 10:00 _____ night.

C Write true sentences about yourself. Look at Exercise B as an example.

I get up _____

_____

_____

_____

D Make questions using *when*, *what time*, and *what day*.

1. Q: What time do you eat breakfast? _____

   A: I eat breakfast at 7:00 in the morning.

2. Q: _____

   A: I leave home at 9 o'clock.

3. Q: _____

   A: I have violin lessons on Mondays.

4. Q: _____

   A: The store opens at 5:00.

5. Q: _____

   A: New Year's Day is on January 1st.

6. Q: _____

   A: Valentine's Day is on February 14th.

7. Q: _____

   A: Christmas is on Thursday.

8. Q: _____

   A: Valentine's Day is on Friday.

E Rewrite the sentences with prepositions of time.

1.

   They eat pizza. (Fridays)

   → They eat pizza on Fridays. _____

2.

   I always feel tired. (the morning)

   → _____

3.

   Linda finished high school. (1998)

   → _____

4.

   We don't go out. (night)

   → _____

A Look at the example and practice with a partner. Use the cues given. (Repeat 3 times.)

I.

 Does Tom take exercise in the evening?

 No, he doesn't. He takes exercise in the morning.

I.

Tom / take exercise / the evening?
→ No / the morning

2.

Kelly / go jogging / Sundays?
→ No / Saturdays

3.

it / snow / August?
→ No / December

4.

Yena / eat hamburgers / lunchtime?
→ No / sandwiches / lunchtime

B Work with a partner. These programs are on TV this weekend. One student chooses a program without telling his/her partner. The partner asks questions to find out what the program is.

		Saturday		Sunday
Morning	9:00	Cinderella	8:00	Magic Show
	12:00	Hello Kitty	10:00	The Jungle Book
Afternoon	2:00	Music Show	3:00	The Love House
	4:00	Sunny Days	4:00	Day by Day
Evening	7:00	Soccer Game	6:00	The News
	9:00	The News	10:00	The Movie: *Transformer*

E.g. (One student chooses The Love House)

Is it on Saturday?
Is it on Sunday?
Is it in the afternoon?
Is it at 3 o'clock?
It's The Love House.

No, it isn't.
Yes, it is.
Yes, it is.
Yes, it is.
Correct! Your turn now.

Unit 16 Adjectives

• Read and answer the questions.
1. What are they doing in the picture?
2. How do they look?
3. What do you do at lunch break?

Unit Focus

▶ Use of Adjectives
▶ Adjective + Noun
▶ Be + Adjective

It is a **beautiful** day. The sky is **blue**. The air is **clean**. Tom and Olivia are having lunch in a **quiet** restaurant. The food is **delicious**. She is holding a **coffee** cup. She looks **happy**.

Learn & Practice 1

Use of Adjectives

- An adjective is a describing word. It tells us more about a noun: number, color, size, shape, feeling, look, condition, sound, smell, etc.

Ava has **long** hair.
She is a **pretty** girl.
She is **pretty**.

It's a **round** table.
It's a **small** table.
It's a **brown** table.

Color		
red	green	white
brown	black	blue

Size		
big	small	tall
short	long	

Feeling		
happy	sad	angry
nice	good	tired

Shape	
round	square

Look		
beautiful	pretty	cute
ugly	old	young
fat	thin	

Number
one, two, three, four, five . . .

Ⓐ Find the adjective in each sentence and write it in the blank.

1. This is an old car. → _____old_____

2. She is a happy woman. → _____

3. You are a nice person. → _____

4. She has a beautiful smile. → _____

5. My sister is smart. → _____

6. You look tired. → _____

7. Laura has brown eyes. → _____

8. They live in a new house. → _____

Adjective + Noun

- We can put adjectives before nouns. Adjectives do not change for singular or plural.
- A noun can be used as an adjective before another noun. The noun that describes another noun is always singular, just like an adjective.

Ashley is a **pretty** girl.
She has **brown** hair.
She has **beautiful** eyes.

They sat at the **kitchen** table.

He is in the **computer** room.

A Underline and write the adjective and noun.

	Adjective	Noun
1. My brother has a <u>big house</u>.	big	house
2. Jason has an expensive bicycle.		
3. The farmers live in small villages.		
4. What is your favorite food?		
5. I want to have a new jacket.		
6. I had an interesting experience today.		

B What are the following objects? Complete the nouns with the words in the box.

paper	key	note	light

1. _note_ pad

2. _____ bulb

3. _____ ring

4. _____ clips

Be + Adjective

- Adjectives can also come after the verb *be* and some other linking verbs like *seem*, *look*, *smell*, *feel*, *taste*, and *sound*. Adjectives describe the subject of the sentence.
- We usually make adjectives of nationality from the name of the country. We must always write the country mames and their adjectives with a capital letter.

He is **young**. He is **happy**.
He is **thin**. He is **Brazilian**.
He is from Brazil.

Country	Adjective	Country	Adjective
Italy	Italian	Australia	Australian
Korea	Korean	Brazil	Brazilian
Japan	Japanese	Canada	Canadian
France	French	China	Chinese
Germany	German	England	English
the USA	American	Russia	Russian
Egypt	Egyptian	Portugal	Portuguese

A Look at the pictures and fill in the blanks.

1.

(cheap / expensive)

The car is ___expensive___.

2.

(happy / angry)

They look _____.

3.

(fast / slow)

The turtle is _____.

4.

(bitter / spicy)

Korean food tastes _____.

5.

(lazy / sad)

What's wrong?
You look _____.

6.

(strong / weak)

He is _____.

B Complete the sentences as in the example.

1. She is from Australia. She is ___Australian___. 2. She is from Brazil. She is _____.

3. He is from England. He is _____. 4. We are from China. We are _____.

5. They are from Canada. They are _____. 6. I am from France. I am _____.

A Correct and rewrite the sentences.

1. The food delicious smells good. → *The delicious food smells good.*

2. What is food favorite your? → _____

3. The elephant lives on the plains hot in Africa. → _____

4. There are pyramids famous in Egypt. → _____

5. Cindy is wearing pink dress her. → _____

B Make sentences about Natalia (1-5) and William (6-10). Use *is/isn't* and one of the adjectives in brackets.

Name: Natalia
Nationality: Portuguese
Marital Status: single
Job: university student
Height: 160 cm
Weight: 46 kilos

Name: William
Nationality: American
Marital Status: married
Job: company employee
Height: 184 cm
Weight: 130 kilos

1. (Spanish / Portuguese) → *Natalia isn't Spanish. She is Portuguese.*

2. (tall / short) → _____

3. (single / married) → _____

4. (old / young) → _____

5. (fat / thin) → _____

6. (Canadian / American) → _____

7. (doctor / company employee) → _____

8. (thin / fat) → _____

9. (short / tall) → _____

10. (married / single) → _____

C Rewrite the sentences so that the adjectives come after the verb *be*.

1. I have a brown bag. → _My bag is brown._

2. This is an expensive ring. → _____

3. John has a big house. → _____

4. That is a tiny insect. → _____

D Complete the sentences with the nouns from the box.

car	house	vegetable	baseball

1. This bat hits baseballs. It is a _____ _baseball bat_ _____.

2. This key is used to start the car. It is my _____.

3. These are my slippers that I wear in the house.
   They are my _____.

4. The soup has vegetables in it. It is a _____.

E Describe each picture using the adjectives in the box.

happy	tired	sad	bored	young	short	straight	
dark brown	curly	angry	good	nice	pretty	black	small

She looks happy.

_____   _____

_____   _____

_____   _____

_____   _____

A Look at the example and practice with a partner. Use the cues given. (Repeat 3 times.)

1.

> Is the woman fat?
>
> No, she isn't. She is thin.

1. the woman / fat?
→ No / thin

2. those boxes / heavy?
→ No / light

3. the man / diligent?
→ No / lazy

4. the airplane / small?
→ No / big

5. the schoolbag / white?
→ No / black

B Work with a partner. Ask questions each other and complete.

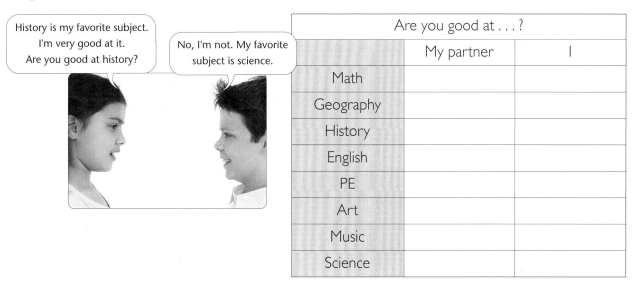

> History is my favorite subject. I'm very good at it. Are you good at history?

> No, I'm not. My favorite subject is science.

Are you good at . . . ?		
	My partner	I
Math		
Geography		
History		
English		
PE		
Art		
Music		
Science		

Unit 17 Adverbs

• Read and answer the questions
1. Where is William?
2. Is William wearing a baseball cap?
3. How often do you exercise?
4. What is the man's job in this picture?

Unit Focus

▶ Meaning & Uses of Adverbs
▶ Rules to Form Adverbs
▶ Adverbs of Frequency

William is a racing driver.
He is young and famous. He's got a fast car.
It is very fast. Racing drivers never drive
slowly. They drive very fast.
They always wear crash helmets.

Learn & Practice 1

Meaning & Uses of Adverbs

- Adverbs tell more about verbs, adjectives, and other adverbs.
- An adverb usually answers to the questions *how*, *where*, or *when*. Adverbs usually go after verbs.

Modifying Verbs	Modifying Adjectives	Modifying Adverbs
The girls sang **loudly**.	I'm **really** nervous.	They drive **very** fast.
My mom gets up **early**.	This T-shirt is **too** big for me.	She swims **quite** well.

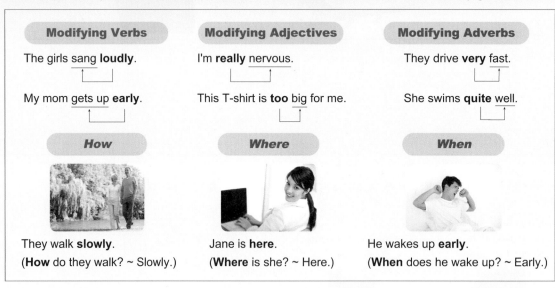

How	**Where**	**When**
They walk **slowly**.	Jane is **here**.	He wakes up **early**.
(**How** do they walk? ~ Slowly.)	(**Where** is she? ~ Here.)	(**When** does he wake up? ~ Early.)

Ⓐ Write the words that the adverbs in bold modify.

1. Joe played **badly** in the hocky match. → _played_

2. He plays tennis **well**. → _____

3. This house is **quite** big. → _____

4. They entered the house **very** quietly. → _____

5. This is a **completely** wrong answer. → _____

B Circle the adverbs and write *tells how*, *tells where*, or *tells when*.

1. She dances (beautifully.) → _tells how_

2. Tom is coming here. → _____

3. I don't get up early on Sundays. → _____

4. The van driver shouted angrily at the cyclist. → _____

5. They are playing outside. → _____

Learn & Practice 2

Rules to Form Adverbs

- Usually we add *-ly* to the end of an adjective to make an adverb.

Rules of Adverbs	Adjectives	Adverbs
For most adverbs, we add **-ly** to the adjective.	slow quick beautiful bad loud slow	slow**ly** quick**ly** beautiful**ly** bad**ly** loud**ly** slow**ly**
If the adjective ends in **-y**, change **-y** to **-i** and add **-ly**.	happy easy noisy heavy	happ**ily** eas**ily** nois**ily** heav**ily**
Some adverbs are the **same as the adjective**.	hard fast late early	**hard** **fast** **late** **early**
Some adverbs are **irregular**.	good	**well**

You must not speak **loudly** in public.

She is a good pianist. She plays the piano **well**.

It's raining **heavily**.

A Look and write the adverbs.

1. heavy → _heavily_

2. easy → _____

3. fast → _____

4. quick → _____

5. good → _____

6. slow → _____

7. early → _____

8. real → _____

9. happy → _____

Adverbs of Frequency

- Adverbs of frequency **tell us** how often something happens.
- Adverbs of frequency **go** before the main verb **but** after the verb *be*.

▭▭▭▭▭	always 100%	I **always** do my homework.
▭▭▭▭□	usually 75%	Do you **usually** work so late?
▭▭▭□□	often 50%	Tom **often** listens to the radio.
▭▭□□□	sometimes 25%	Kelly **sometimes** drinks coffee.
□□□□□	never 0%	Penguins **never** fly.

- The adverbs of frequency answer the typical questions starting with "*how often*".

Q: **How often** does your father cook?
A: He **always** cooks.

Q: **How often** do you brush your teeth?
A: I **often** brush my teeth.

A Add the adverb of frequency to each sentence.

1. I am late for work. (always) → _I am always late for work._

2. They eat fast food. (often) → _____

3. We are late for school. (never) → _____

4. They are absent from school. (sometimes) → _____

5. He has breakfast at 7:30. (usually) → _____

A Rewrite the sentences using a verb and an adverb.

1. They're slow workers.
   → _____They work slowly._____

2. She's a bad actress.
   → _____She acts badly._____

3. She's a dangerous driver.
   → _____

4. Ava is a beautiful dancer.
   → _____

5. You're a loud singer.
   → _____

6. They're good teachers.
   → _____

7. He is a careful driver.
   → _____

8. She's a fast swimmer.
   → _____

B How does Olivia get to school? Write the answers.

How do you get to school?				
	walk	take the school bus	ride her bicycle	go by subway
always				
usually	✓			
often		✓		
sometimes			✓	
seldom				
never				✓

1. _Olivia usually walks to school._____

2. _____

3. _____

4. _____

C Fill in the blanks with *good*, *well*, *hard*, and *fast*. Then, write if each is an adjective or an adverb.

1. Jessica is a __good__ singer. She sings very __well__.   Adjective: __good__ Adverb: __well__

2. You must run _____ to catch that last bus.   Adjective: _____ Adverb: _____

3. Tom isn't clever but he tries very _____ at school.   Adjective: _____ Adverb: _____

4. That horse is a _____ runner. It wins every race.   Adjective: _____ Adverb: _____

5. This cake tastes really _____.   Adjective: _____ Adverb: _____

6. My computer doesn't work very _____.   Adjective: _____ Adverb: _____

D What does the girls always do in the morning? Look at the pictures and write a sentence to describe each one.

6:00	6:40	7:00

She always gets up at 6:00 in the morning.

_____

_____

7:20	7:40	8:00

_____

_____

E Read and write the appropriate answers about you. Use *always*, *usually*, *sometimes*, or *never*.

1. How often do you wake up before 7 o'clock?

   I usually wake up before 7 o'clock.

2. What time do you usually eat breakfast?

   _____

3. What time do you get to school?

   _____

4. How often do you eat fruits and vegetables?

   _____

5. How often do you usually exercise?

   _____

6. How often do you take a shower?

   _____

A Look at the example and practice with a partner. Use the cues given. (Repeat 3 times.)

1.

James / shout / quiet?
→ No / loud

1.

Does James shout quietly?

No, he doesn't. He shouts loudly.

2. they / dance / sad?
→ No / happy

3. he / get up / early?
→ No / late

4. the kangaroo / run / slow? → No / fast

5. she / play the violin / bad? → No / good

B Interview! Work with a partner and write. Use *always*, *usually*, *often*, *sometimes*, or *never* to make sentences.

How often do you eat fast food?

I never eat fast food.

How often do you . . .?	
eat fast food?	go swimming?
tidy your room?	go to the movie theater?
work on your computer?	eat meat?
do chores at home?	visit relatives on the weekend?
read poetry?	listen to the radio at night?
do your homework on the bus?	

My partner: _____ (name of your partner)

He (or She) never eats fast food. _____

_____

_____

_____

_____

A Complete these sentences with *at*, *in*, or *on*.

1. She was ___at___ the bus stop for half an hour.

2. I met my girlfriend _____ a party.

3. She usually sits _____ the floor.

4. The painting looks nice _____ this wall.

5. Do you live _____ Manchester?

6. My toothbrush isn't _____ the bathroom.

B Which is right?

1. Don't eat so (quick / (quickly)). It's not good for you.

2. You can learn this language (easy / easily).

3. This is a (slow / slowly) train. It stops everywhere.

4. Kathy is a very (careful / carefully) driver.

5. Some companies pay their workers very (bad / badly).

C Add the frequency adverbs to the sentences below.

1. John goes bicycle riding. (always)

→ _____

2. Benjamin collects stamps. (never)

→ _____

3. Harry plays basketball on Monday morning. (often)

→ _____

4. She is at work on Sundays. (usually)

→ _____

5. Andrea watches TV after work. (sometimes)

→ _____

6. He is in his office. (always)

→ _____

D Complete the sentences using *at*, *in*, or *on*.

1. I left the library ___at___ 8 o'clock last night.

2. We will leave for Singapore _____ Monday, Jan. 25th.

3. Where were you _____ Saturday morning?

4. What do you want to do _____ the evening?

5. We usually go fishing _____ the summer.

6. What time do you go to bed _____ night?

E Look at the information in brackets and put in the adverbs. Be careful with the spelling.

1. (Kelly's toothache was terrible.) → Kelly's tooth ached ___terribly___.

2. (William was angry.) → William shouted _____ at the waiter.

3. (I'm happy sitting here.) → I can sit here _____ for hours.

F Unscramble the words to make questions.

1. the concert? / is / when → _____When is the concert?_____

2. what time / to school? / go / do you / usually → _____

3. usually / do / when / you / get up? → _____

4. do / what time / lunch? / you / eat → _____

G Look at the pictures and complete the answers to each question.

1.

Q: Where is the shoe?

A: _It is under the bed._

2.

Q: Where is the man?

A: _____

3.

Q: Where are the pigs?

A: _____

4.

Q: Where is the man?

A: _____

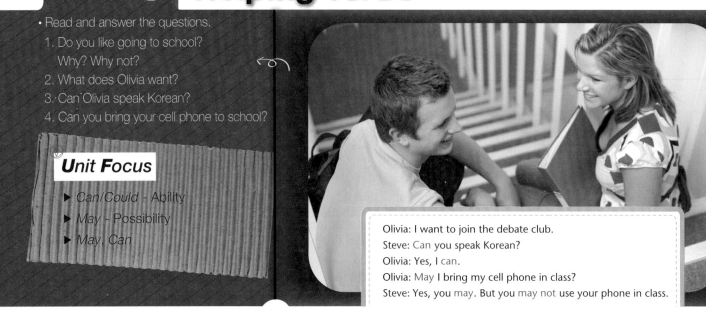

Unit 18 Helping Verbs

- Read and answer the questions.
1. Do you like going to school?
   Why? Why not?
2. What does Olivia want?
3. Can Olivia speak Korean?
4. Can you bring your cell phone to school?

Unit Focus

▶ *Can/Could* - Ability
▶ *May* - Possibility
▶ *May, Can*

Olivia: I want to join the debate club.
Steve: Can you speak Korean?
Olivia: Yes, I can.
Olivia: May I bring my cell phone in class?
Steve: Yes, you may. But you may not use your phone in class.

Learn & Practice 1

Can/Could – Ability

- We use *can* or *can't* (= *cannot*) to talk about ability in the present.
- We use *could* or *couldn't* (= *could not*) to talk about ability in the past.

I **can** write with my left hand.

Peter **could** play tennis last year, but he **can't** play tennis now.

Statements	Negative
He **can** sing.	He **can't** sing.
I **could** play the piano.	I **couldn't** play the piano.

Questions

Can	I/we/you he/she/it/they	drive	. . .?
Could	I/we/you he/she/it/they		. . .?

Answers

Yes, No,	I/we/you he/she/it/they	can. can't.
Yes, No,	I/we/you he/she/it/they	could. couldn't.

Can you speak English? ~ Yes, I **can**.
~ No, I **can't**.

Could he ride a bicycle? ~ Yes, he **could**.
~ No, he **couldn't**.

A Fill in *can*, *can't*, *could*, or *couldn't*.

When I was young, I ___could___ play sports, but I _____ sing well. Now I'm old; I _____

climb the stairs, but I ___can't___ sit in my armchair and watch TV.

B Make *yes/no* questions and write the answers.

1. Tom can play the guitar.   Q: *Can Tom play the guitar?* _____   A: Yes, ___he can___ .

2. She could stand on her head.   Q: _____   A: No, _____ .

3. Kelly could speak Korean.   Q: _____   A: No, _____ .

4. Ava can drive a car.   Q: _____   A: Yes, _____ .

Learn & Practice 2

May – Possibility

- We use *may* to talk about something that it is possible now or in the future.
- We use *will* or the present continuous when we are certain about something. We use *may* when we are not certain.

William **may** arrive late. (It's possible.)

William **will** be late. (It's certain.)

William **isn't coming** tonight. (We know that he won't come.)

Subject	*May*	Base Verb
I/We/You He/She/It/They Tom, etc.	may / may not	go.

A Rewrite the sentences as in the example.

1. She goes to Mexico next year.   → (It's possible.) *She may go to Mexico next year.* _____

2. He is late.   → (It's certain.) _____

3. You have a problem with your car.   → (It's possible.) _____

4. Cities become more crowded.   → (It's certain.) _____

May, Can

- We can use *may* and *can* to give or refuse permission.
- We can also use *May I* and *Can I* to ask permission to do something. *May* is more formal than *can* and we use it when speaking to someone who is older, who is in authority over us, or whom we do not know very well. *Can* is often used between people who know each other well.

You **may** not use my laptop.

May I see your driver's licence?
~ Yes, of course.
(They do not know each other.)

Can I go to the party, Dad?
~ Sure.
(They know each other.)

- We usually say "*Okay*; *Yes, of course*; *Certainly*; *Sure*; or *No problem*. We usually say *I'm sorry, but . . .*; *No, I'm sorry*; or *No, thanks* instead of *No, you may not* (or *can't*).

Ⓐ Fill in *can* or *may*.

1.

_____Can_____ I go fishing with you, Dad?

2.

_____ I introduce you to Mr. Lee?

3.

_____ I use your smartphone?

Ⓑ Read the underlined words and write *possibility* or *permission*.

1. She <u>may</u> go to Singapore next week.   →   _____possibility_____

2. You <u>may</u> use a dictionary during the test.   →   _____

3. <u>Can</u> I borrow your bicycle?   →   _____

4. You <u>can</u> go earlier than usual.   →   _____

5. I don't know. She <u>may</u> visit her grandma.   →   _____

6. She <u>may</u> be in the classroom.   →   _____

A Look at the pictures. Then write sentences about what Emma can or can't do.

I'm Emma.
I'm a student.

1. She can't play volleyball.

2. _____

3. _____

4. _____

1.

play volleyball (X)

2.

eat with chopsticks (O)

3.

make spaghetti (O)

4.

ride a bicycle (X)

B George was at home last week with a broken leg. What could he do? What couldn't he do? Write sentences using the words and expressions below.

read comic books   listen to music

play soccer   swim

run around on the playground   watch TV

1. He couldn't play soccer.   2. _____

3. _____   4. _____

5. _____   6. _____

C Write four things you couldn't do before, but you can do now.

1. Three years ago, I couldn't whistle, but I can whistle well now.

2. _____

3. _____

4. _____

D Read the situations. Make questions with *May I . . .?* or *Can I . . .?* as in the example.

1. You want to borrow your friend's pencil. What do you say to him?
   → *Can I borrow your pencil, please?* _____

2. You want to use the phone in your teacher's office. What do you say to her?
   → _____

3. You want to go shopping with your mother. What do you say to your mother?
   → _____

4. You want to go to the party. What do you say to your father?
   → _____

5. You want to borrow the digital camera in your boss's office. What do you say to him?
   → _____

E Rewrite the sentences with *may.*

1. Perhaps we'll go out.   → *We may go out.* _____

2. Perhaps she will come tomorrow.   → _____

3. I don't know if we'll get an invitation.   → _____

4. I'm not sure if my friends are visiting me.   → _____

5. Perhaps I'll go to the movie theater this weekend. → _____

F Make *yes/no* questions. Then, write the correct answers.

1. Q: *Can Bob speak French?* _____

   A: *No, he can't.* _____ Bob / speak French (✗)

2. Q: Can Sunny climb trees?

   A: _____ Sunny / climb trees (○)

3. Q: Can Nancy play badminton?

   A: _____ Nancy / play badminton (✗)

4. Q: Can Brian run very fast?

   A: _____ Brian / run very fast (✗)

A Look at the example and practice with a partner. Use the cues given. (Repeat 3 times.)

1.

I / bring / my lunch?
→ Yes / But / eat / in class

 Can I bring my lunch?

 Yes, you can bring your lunch.
But you can't eat in class.

2.

I / run / outside?
→ Yes / But / run / in the hallways

3.

I / bring / my cell phone / to school?
→ Yes / But / use your phone / in class

4.

I / have / my MP3 player / in school?
→ Yes / But / listen to music / in class

5.

I / wear / earrings / in school?
→ Yes / But / wear bracelets / in school

B Work with a partner. Ask questions and answer them using *can*. Then ask, "*How about you?*"

Can Lucy speak English?

No, she can't, but she can speak Korean. How about you?

I can speak Portuguese.

Lucy: speak English → No / Korean

Nick: play soccer → No / tennis

Eric: ride a horse → No / a bicycle

Hannah: swim → No / float on water

Alice: write stories → No / take photos

Helping Verbs 123

- Read and answer the questions.
  1. Where are they?
  2. What are they doing in the picture?
  3. You have a little brother. He's going into the sea after eating. What do you say?
  4. Should we wear a hat at the beach? Why?

Unit Focus

▶ Imperatives
▶ Suggestion: *Let's*

How to stay safe at the beach!
It's holiday time. Let's go to the beach. Don't swim after eating. Wear a hat. It protects your head and your eyes from the sun. Don't go out in the sun between 11 a.m. and 3 p.m. Drink plenty of water. Always put sun cream on your skin to protect your skin from the hot sun!

Learn & Practice 1

Imperatives

- The imperative is the only form that doesn't need to carry a subject.
- We form the affirmative imperative with the base form of the verb (*close*, *sit*, *be*, etc.).
- We form the negative imperative with *don't* + base form of the verb.

To Give Instructions	**To Give Orders or Tell People What To Do**

Bend to the right.　**Don't** talk.　　**Don't** move.　　**Stand** at attention.

To Give Advice	**To Give Encouragement**	**To Make Requests**

Get some rest.　　**Never give up.**　**Always do** your best.　　**Come in, please.**
Please close the door.

＊We use the imperative to give encouragement. We can put *always* and *never* before an imperative.

＊With the addition of *please*, imperative sentences are used to make polite requests.

A Look at the pictures. Choose and complete the sentences.

Don't smoke   Turn off   Be quiet

1.
Your are in the library.

_____, please.

2.
You are on the plane.

_____ here.

3.
The movie is starting.

_____ your

cell phone.

B Read and circle the correct word.

1. (Be)/ Don't) quiet in class.

2. (Turns / Turn) off the TV.

3. (Close / Be close) the window.

4. (Doesn't / Don't) call me before 11 o'clock.

5. (Watch / Watches) out! There's a bee on your nose.

6. (Open you / Open) your books to page 10.

C Look at the sentences A and B. Then follow the instructions.

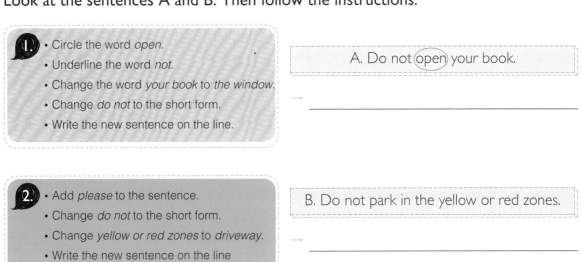

1.
- Circle the word *open*.
- Underline the word *not*.
- Change the word *your book* to *the window*.
- Change *do not* to the short form.
- Write the new sentence on the line.

A. Do not (open) your book.

_____

2.
- Add *please* to the sentence.
- Change *do not* to the short form.
- Change *yellow or red zones* to *driveway*.
- Write the new sentence on the line

B. Do not park in the yellow or red zones.

_____

Let's

- We use *let's* + the base verb to make a suggestion for two or more people. *Let's* includes the speaker.
- *Let's* is a contraction of *let* + *us*, but we usually say and write *let's*.
- The negative form is *let's not* + base verb.

Let's + Base Verb	**Let's + Not + Base Verb**
A: I love going to the movie theater.	A: It is a rainy day.
B: OK. **Let's** go to the movie theater.	B: **Let's not** play tennis.

A Match the answers with *let's* or *let's not* to the following statements.

1. The concert starts in a few minutes.   a. Let's not go by car.

2. Gasoline is too expensive.   b. Let's not stay at home.

3. We have a test tomorrow.   c. Let's go to the library and study.

4. It's a lovely day.   d. Let's not be late.

B Make sentences with *let's* or *let's not*.

1. A: We need to get some groceries.   B: _____Let's go to the supermarket._____
    (go to the supermarket)

2. A: We have a test tomorrow.   B: _____
    (watch a movie)

3. A: It's Ava's birthday next week.   B: _____
    (buy her a present)

4. A: It's cold. We can't swim today.   B: _____
    (go to the beach)

A Match the sentences with the pictures. What does the imperative show in each picture: *order*, *instruction*, or *suggestion*?

> Don't move! You're under arrest.   Please sign your name at the bottom.   Let's read the map.

1.

Please sign your name at the bottom.

→ instruction

2.

_____

→ _____

3.

_____

→ _____

B Fill in the gaps with one of the verbs from the box. Use each verb only once. Which sentence needs *don't*? Which needs *let's (not)*? Which only needs the verb?

> play   watch   stay   wash   be   move   close   have   turn on

1. We're bored. ___Let's play___ a game.

2. Always _____ your hands before you sit at the table.

3. It's our anniversary next week. _____ a party.

4. _____ late! Your teacher will be angry.

5. _____! There's a bee on your nose.

6. It's getting dark. _____ the light, please.

7. Next Monday is a holiday. _____ at home.

8. It's too late to go to the movie theater now. _____ a video instead.

9. I'm cold. _____ the windows, please.

C Read and rewrite the sentences with *let's*.

1. Why don't we go to the beach? → Let's go to the beach.

2. Why don't we go to a soccer game? → _____

3. Why don't we leave at six thirty? → _____

4. Why don't we eat out for dinner? → _____

5. Why don't we send Harry an email? → _____

D Make an imperative sentence for each of the following situations.

1. You're in a restaurant. You want some more coffee.

→ Please give me some more coffee. _____ (me / give)

2. You're in a school bus. You want the driver to stop at the bookstore.

→ _____ (in front of)

3. You are a doctor. You have a patient with cough and fever. You want to advise something.

→ _____ (a lot of water / and / take / drink / a rest)

4. You're a teacher. It's cold and windy outside. You want a student to close the window.

→ _____ (close)

E Give advice to a friend in these situations. Use affirmative and negative imperatives.

1. I have a cold.

→ Don't go to school. Don't go outside. Stay at home and take a rest. Drink lots of tea with lemon.

2. I can't speak English very well.

→ _____

3. I can't fall asleep at night.

→ _____

4. I have a test tomorrow.

→ _____

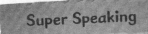

Super Speaking

A Look at the example and practice with a partner. Use the words below or invent your own. (Repeat 3 times.)

1.

 It's a lovely day today. Let's go for a walk.

 No, let's not. Why don't we go to the beach?

 Sounds good! What a good idea!

1. go for a walk
→ No / go to the beach?

2. go swimming
→ No / go fishing?

3. walk downtown
→ No / get a cup of coffee?

4. go shopping
→ No / go to a movie theater?

5. go to the Seoul Tower
→ No / go to a seafood restaurant?

B Tell your partner what to do / not to do in the classroom. Use the verbs below.

write eat talk
play listen
sleep
shout dance

Don't write on the walls!

Write in your notebook!

Questions: the Verb *Be*

• Read and answer the questions.

1. Was Bruno at the library last night?
2. Why is Bruno angry?
3. Where were you yesterday afternoon?
4. What are you interested in?

Unit *Focus*

▶ *Yes/No* Questions
▶ Information Questions with the Verb *Be*

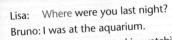

Lisa: Where were you last night?
Bruno: I was at the aquarium.
Lisa: Are you interested in watching movies?
Bruno: No, I'm not. I'm interested in singing theses days.
Lisa: Why are you angry?
Bruno: I am angry because I failed math.

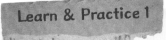

Learn & Practice 1

Yes/No Questions: The Verb *Be* (Present, Past)

- To make *yes/no* questions, we put the verb *be* before the subject. *Yes/No* questions end with a question mark (?).

- We use *was* and *were* to talk about situations that happened in the past.

Present	Past

Q: **Is** he a soccer player?	Q: **Was** Marilyn Monroe a painter?
A: **No**, he **isn't**. He **is** a tennis player.	A: **No**, she **wasn't**. She **was** a famous actress.

Be	Subject	. . .?	Short Answers	
Am	I		Yes, I am.	No, I'm not.
Was			Yes, I was.	No, I wasn't.
Is	he/she/it	happy?	Yes, he is.	No, he isn't.
Was			Yes, she was.	No, she wasn't.
Are	you/we/they		Yes, we are.	No, we aren't.
Were			Yes, they were.	No, they weren't.

A Use the words to ask a *yes/no* question.

1. Nancy / from Canada. → *Is Nancy from Canada?*

2. you / at home yesterday → _____

3. I / late for class → _____

4. we / busy two days ago → _____

5. they / in class yesterday → _____

6. Peter / at home last night → _____

Learn & Practice 2

Information Questions with the Verb *Be*

- Question words go at the beginning of the question, followed by the verb and the subject.
- We use *what* to ask questions about things. We use *where* to ask questions about location. We use *who* to ask questions about people. We use *when* for questions about time. We use *how* to ask questions about people's health or happiness. We use *why* to ask questions about reasons.

Q: **What** are they?
A: They are doves.

Q: **Where** were you?
A: I was in the library.

Q: **How** are they?
A: They are happy.

Q: **Why** were you late?
A: I got up late.

＊We use '*What is he/she?*' to ask a question about his/her job.   E.g. *What is she? ~ She is a doctor.*

WH- Word	Be	Subject	...?	Answers
What	was	she?		She was an actress.
Where	is	Joe?		He is at home.
Who	is	she?		She is my girlfriend.
When	were	you	there?	I was there three years ago.
How	was	she	last night?	She was very sick.
Why	is	Kathy	happy?	Because she is going to the beach.

A Write *what, where, when, who, why,* or *how.* Then circle the correct verb.

1.

   Q: _What_ is it?

   A: It (is)/ are) a book.

2.

   Q: _____ is Jane?

   A: She (are / is) at home.

3.

   Q: _____ is she?

   A: She (was / is) my mother.

4.

   Q: _____ is your birthday?

   A: It (is / was) on Saturday.

5.

   Q: _____ are your parents?

   A: They (were / are) fine.

6.

   Q: _____ are you angry?

   A: Because you (were / are) late.

B Read the answers. Then write *wh-* questions with *be.*

1.

   _What is she_____?

   She is a doctor.

2.

   _____?

   It is a car.

3.

   _____?

   They were in the library.

4.

   _____?

   They are happy.

A Write questions and answers as in the example.

1.

Q: Are they teachers?

A: No, they aren't. They are dancers.

teachers? → No / dancers

2.

Q: _____

A: _____

a police officer? → No / a waiter

3.

Q: _____

A: _____

apples? → No / tomatoes

B Write questions about famous people from the past. Then write answers to the questions.

1. Napoleon / a musician
   → No / a good leader

   Q: Was Napoleon a musician?

   A: No, he wasn't. He was a good leader.

2. Leonardo da Vinci / an explorer
   → No / a famous painter

   Q: _____

   A: _____

3. Andre Kim / Japanese
   → No / Korean

   Q: _____

   A: _____

4. The Beatles / French
   → No / English

   Q: _____

   A: _____

5. Cleopatra / Brazilian
   → No / Egyptian

   Q: _____

   A: _____

6. Elvis Presley / an astronaut
   → No / a famous singer

   Q: _____

   A: _____

C Read the answers. Then write *wh-* questions with *be*.

1.

Q: Where is your bicycle?

A: My bicycle is in the park.

2.

Q: _____

A: Christmas is on December 25th.

3.

Q: _____

A: They were at school yesterday.

4.

Q: _____

A: Halloween is on October 31st.

D Answer these questions about yourself.

1. Where were you born?

→ _____

2. What is your father?

→ _____

3. When was your last birthday?

→ _____

4. Who are you?

→ _____

5. What are your hobbies?

→ _____

6. How are you?

→ _____

A Look at the example and practice with a partner. Use the words below or invert your own. (Repeat 3 times.)

1.

at home now? → Yes
in Egypt last year?
→ No / in Seoul

 Are you at home now?

 Yes, I am.

 Were you in Egypt last year?

 No, I wasn't. I was in Seoul.

2.

tired now? → Yes
sad yesterday?
→ No / nervous

3.

in class now? → Yes
in the library last night?
→ No / at the aquarium

4.

at home now? → Yes
at the parking lot
yesterday afternoon?
→ No / at work

5.

in Paris now? → Yes
in Singapore last
summer?
→ No / in Thailand

B Work with a partner. Ask and answer questions.

Tom / at the library last night?
→ No / at a party

 Your turn now.

Was Tom at the library last night? Where was he?

No, he wasn't. He was at a party.

Jane / at home yesterday?
→ No / at work

Paul and Ava / at the park last night?
→ No / at the movie theater

Kelly / at the park yesterday afternoon?
→ No / at the train station

Bob / at the grocery store yesterday?
→ No / at the restaurant

Questions: Action Verbs

- Read and answer the questions.
1. Does Patrick wear glasses?
2. Where does Patrick work?
3. What did you do last weekend?
4. Where did you go on vacation?

A: What does Patrick do?
B: He's a student, and he has a part-time job.
A: Where does he work?
B: He works in a restaurant.
A: Did he work yesterday?
B: No, he didn't.
A: What did he do yesterday?
B: He played tennis with his father.

Unit Focus

▶ Yes/No Questions
▶ Information Questions with Action Verbs
▶ Questions with *Who* and *What* as the Subject

Learn & Practice 1

Yes/No Questions: Present, Past

- We use *do*, *does*, or *did* to make questions. We put them before the subject and always use the base verb.

Present	Past

Q: **Does** Olivia jog every morning?	Q: **Did** you finish your homework?
A: **Yes**, she **does**.	A: **No**, I **didn't**.
Q: **Does** she wear glasses?	Q: **Did** you enjoy last weekend?
A: **No**, she **doesn't**.	A: **Yes**, I **did**.

Do/Does/Did	Subject	Base Verb	Short Answers	
Do	I/you/we they		Yes, I do. Yes, they do.	No, I don't. No, they don't.
Does	he/she/it Tom, etc.	work?	Yes, he does. Yes, she does.	No, he doesn't. No, she doesn't.
Did	All Subjects		Yes, we did. Yes, it did.	No, we didn't. No, it didn't.

A Read each sentence and make questions.

1. She eats vegetables every day.　　→　*Does she eat vegetables every day?*

2. He likes French fries.　　→　_____

3. They got married 15 years ago.　　→　_____

4. Kathy went to school yesterday.　　→　_____

5. She visited her grandmother.　　→　_____

6. Ben talked on the phone to his friend.　　→　_____

Learn & Practice 2

Information Questions with Action Verbs

- We use *WH-* question words to get information. We put the question words before *do, does,* and *did*.

- We use *what* to ask questions about things. We use *when* for questions about time. We use *where* to ask questions about location. We use *why* to ask questions about reasons. We use *who* to ask questions about people. We use *how* to ask questions about the way of doing things.

Q: **What** do architects do?
A: They design buildings.

Q: **Where** did you go on vacation?
A: I went to the beach.

Q: **Why** did you stay home?
A: Because I didn't feel well.

WH- Word	Do/Did/Does	Subject	Base Verb
What	do	I	do?
When	did	you	go to the beach?
Where	did	she	stay?
Why	does	he	get up early?
Who	does	Jane	love?
How	did	you	go?

A Look and make questions as in the example.

1. Penguins eat. + what → What do penguins eat?

2. They lived. + where → _____

3. You stayed home. + why → _____

4. You get to work. + how → _____

5. She likes for dessert. + what → _____

Learn & Practice 3

Questions with *Who* and *What* as the Subject

- When *who* and *what* are the subject of a sentence, we do not need the auxiliary verb. **Who did you meet?** The subject is **you**, so it is necessary. But in **Who came yesterday?** the subject is **who**, so we do not need the auxiliary verb.

Michelle saw Brian.

Who saw Brian? (*Who* is the subject.)

~ Michelle. (Michelle saw him.)

Who did Michelle see? (*Who* is the object.)

~ Brian. (She saw Brian.)

WH- Word as Subject	Present/Past Tense Verb
Who	rang you?
What	will happen next?

A Write questions with *who* or *what*. In these questions, *who/what* is the subject.

1. Somebody broke the glasses. → Who broke the glasses?

2. Something fell off the tree. → _____

3. Somebody took my wallet. → _____

4. Something made me happy. → _____

5. Somebody lives in this house. → _____

A Look and make questions for each answer.

1.

Q: How do you go _____ to school?

A: By school bus. (I go to school by school bus.)

2.

Q: _____ every day?

A: At the cafeteria. (Sunny eats lunch at the cafeteria every day.)

3.

Q: _____?

A: At 8:00. (The movie starts at 8:00.)

4.

Q: _____?

A: Because it's important. (I study English because it's important.)

5.

Q: _____?

A: In Australia. (Kangaroos live in Australia.)

B Read each answer. Write a *yes/no* question with the words in parentheses and a short negative answer.

1. Q: Did she have a fever? _____ (she / fever)

   A: No, _____ she didn't _____ . She had a cold.

2. Q: _____ (Peter / at the post office)

   A: No, _____ . He works at the library.

3. Q: _____ (Nancy / shopping)

   A: No, _____ . She went fishing.

4. Q: _____ (Marco / at a restaurant)

   A: No, _____ . He eats lunch at a cafeteria every day.

5. Q: _____ (he / Monday)

   A: No, _____ . He exercised on Friday.

C Write questions with *who* or *what* (subject or object).

1. I eat something. → *What do you eat?*

2. Someone knocked on the door. → *Who knocked on the door?*

3. Something happened last night. → _____

4. Somebody did the dishes. → _____

5. You were talking to someone. → _____

6. This word means something. → _____

7. Lisa learned something. → _____

D Look at the picture and write questions for the answers. Use the underlined words to help you choose the correct question word.

1. *Who did you see?* _____
   → I saw Olivia.

2. *When did you see her?* _____
   → I saw her yesterday afternoon.

3. _____
   → I saw her in a cafe.

4. _____
   → She looked happy.

5. _____
   → She said hello.

6. _____
   → She read the newspaper.

7. _____
   → She came home at 11 p.m.

A Look at the example and practice with a partner. Use the words below or invent your own. (Repeat 3 times.)

1.

your sister (a journalist)
a TV station / I (an actor)

2.

your father (a business manager)
an office / I (teacher)

3.

your brother (a waiter)
a restaurant / I
(computer programmer)

4.

your mother
(salesperson)
a store / I (police officer)

5.

your aunt (an actress)
a theater / I (doctor)

1.

 What does your sister do?

 She is a journalist.

 Where does she work?

 She works in a TV station.

 What do you want to be?

 I want to be an actor.

B Work with a partner. What did you do last summer? Ask and answer questions as in the example.

Where did you go on vacation?
What did you do?
What did your father do?
Your turn now.

I went to the beach.
I took some photos.
He swam every day.

go shopping	travel abroad	swim every day	go hiking every day
	stay at a hotel	sunbathe in the mornings	go fishing
meet some new people	watch the sunset	read a lot of books	collect some shells

A Steve is 70 years old. What could he do when he was young, but can't do now? Make sentences using the prompts below as in the example.

1. play soccer
2. dance all night
3. eat a lot
4. walk for miles
5. lift heavy things

1. He could play soccer but now he can't.

2. _____

3. _____

4. _____

5. _____

B Read the situations. Make questions with *May I* or *Can I* as in the example.

1. You want to borrow your friend's dictionary. What do you say to him?

→ Can I borrow your dictionary, please?

2. You want to use the laptop in your boss's office. What do you say to him (or her)?

→ _____

3. You want to invite some friends to dinner. What do you say to your mother?

→ _____

C Look at the pictures and the prompts. Write questions and answers, as in the example.

1.

What / Lucy / do / after school?
(do one's homework)

Q: What does Lucy do after school?

A: She does her homework.

2.

What / Steve / do / in the afternoon?
(go skateboarding)

Q: _____

A: _____

3.

Where / they / go / every Saturday?
(go to a seafood restaurant)

Q: _____

A: _____

4.

How / they / get to school?
(usually walk)

Q: _____

A: _____

D **Read each statement. First write a *yes/no* question with the words in parentheses. Then write a short answer.**

1. I was tired yesterday. (you) Q: *Were you tired yesterday?* A: No, ___*I wasn't*___.

2. They were nervous. (Jane) Q: _____ A: Yes, _____.

3. Lisa is with the dog. (they) Q: _____ A: No, _____.

4. You were at the dentist's. (he) Q: _____ A: Yes, _____.

5. Are you married? (she) Q: _____ A: No, _____.

E **Write a *yes/no* question about the past with *Did... last weekend?*. Then write a short answer.**

1. (Ava / email a friend) Q: *Did Ava email a friend last weekend?* A: No, ___*she didn't*___.

2. (you / wear a new T-shirt) Q: _____ A: Yes, _____.

3. (Tom / buy a new CD) Q: _____ A: No, _____.

4. (they / watch a movie) Q: _____ A: Yes, _____.

F **Complete the sentences with the imperative form of the verb in the box.**

go	sit	relax	review

Study a little every day. Don't ___*review*___ everything in one day. _____ in a quiet room. Study for thirty minutes and then have a rest for five minutes. _____ to bed early before the exam. Don't get nervous. _____ before the test.

G **Read and rewrite the sentences with *let's*.**

1. Why don't we go to a seafood restaurant? → *Let's go to a seafood restaurant.*

2. Why don't we go to a movie? → _____

3. Why don't we go to the beach? → _____

H **Write questions for the answers. Use the underlined words to help you choose the correct question word.**

1. *Who did you see?* ~ I saw William.

2. _____ ~ William had a bad day yesterday.

3. _____ ~ He felt tired.

4. _____ ~ He came home at 10 p.m.

You are my
Grammar &
Speaking

1 Student Book

Answer Key

Unit 1
Simple Present of *Be*
p. 8

Learn & Practice 1

A 1. are 2. is 3. are 4. is 5. are 6. am

Learn & Practice 2

A 1. Your shoes aren't very dirty.
   2. They aren't good basketball players.
   3. The bank isn't open today.
   4. We aren't interested in football.

Learn & Practice 3

A 1. Are; they are 2. Is; she isn't 3. Are; I am
   4. Is; it isn't

Learn & Practice 4

A 1. There are 2. There is

B 1. There isn't a table in the kitchen.
   2. Is there a telephone on the table?
   3. There aren't buses on the street.
   4. Are there five floors in this building?

Super Writing

A 1. isn't; He is a photographer.
   2. isn't; He is a bus driver.
   3. isn't; She is a doctor.
   4. aren't; They are from Korea.

B 1. Q: Is Canada a city?   A: No, it isn't. It is a country.
   2. Q: Is Africa a city?   A: No, it isn't. It is a continent.
   3. Q: Are Beijing and London countries?
      A: No, they aren't. They are cities.

C 1. There is a girl at the table.
   2. There is a laptop.
   3. There is a pen holder.
   4. There is an apple.
   5. There are some books.
   6. There are glasses.
   7. There are some notebooks.
   8. There are some color pencils.

E ① Is she ② she isn't ③ architect ④ Is she
   ⑤ No, she isn't ⑥ is an English

Unit 2
Simple Present 1
p. 14

Learn & Practice 1

A 1. teaches 2. lives 3. rings 4. work 5. eats
   6. drives

Learn & Practice 2

A 1. catches 2 eats 3. has 4. loves 5. speaks
   6. guesses 7. sees 8. studies 9. flies

B 1. catches 2. teaches 3. bakes

Learn & Practice 3

A 1. doesn't 2 don't 3. don't 4. doesn't
   5. doesn't 6. don't

B 1. doesn't want 2. doesn't eat 3. doesn't drink
   4. doesn't like

Super Writing

A 1. Maria brushes her teeth before breakfast.
   2. Edward reads books on the weekenD
   3 They watch DVDs in the evenings.

B 1. doesn't drink coffee; She drinks milk.
   2. doesn't watch sports on TV; She plays badminton.
   3. doesn't like vegetables; He likes hamburgers.
   4. doesn't have cats; She has a small puppy.

C 1. The sun doesn't rise in the west. The sun (= It)
      rises in the east.
   2. The sun doesn't go around the earth. The earth
      goes around the sun.
   3. Penguins don't live in Africa. Penguins (= They) live
      in the Antarctic.
   4. A teacher doesn't work in a hospital. A teacher
      (= He/She) works in a school.

D 1. washes plates and cups
   2. makes food hot
   3. keep food very cold
   4. keeps food cool
   5. wash clothes
   6. copies of papers
   7. takes photographs

Unit 3

Simple Present 2

p. 20

Learn & Practice 1
A 1. Does; does 2. Do; don't 3. Does; does

Learn & Practice 2
A 1. does; work 2. do; go 3. does; live
   4. does; come
B 1. Where does 2. Where does 3. Where does
   4. Where does 5. Where do 6. Where does

Learn & Practice 3
A 1. does 2. do 3. does 4. do 5. buy 6. mean
B 1. What do you want for lunch?
   2. What do you do in your free time?
   3. What does this word mean?
   4. What do kangaroos eat?
   5. What does your dad do in the morning?

Super Writing
A 1. Q: Does she drink coffee?
      A: No, she doesn't. She drinks tea.
   2. Q: Does Olivia ride a skateboard?
      A: No, she doesn't. She rides a bicycle.
   3. Q: Does kathy have a camera?
      A: No, she doesn't. She has a laptop.
   4. Q: Does he do exercise?
      A: Yes, he does.
B 1. What does Cindy do after school?
      She does her homework.
   2. Where do they eat lunch every day?
      They eat lunch at the cafeteria every day.
   3. What does Tom do in the afternoon?
      He goes skateboarding.
   4. Where do your parents go every Saturday?
      They go to a seafood restaurant.
C 1. Does Lucy like apple pie?
      No, she doesn't. She likes potato chips and pizza.
   2. Do Lucy and Mark like pizza?
      Yes, they do.
   3. Does Mark go to the library on the weekend?
      No, he doesn't. He goes to the bookstore.
   4. Does Lucy play soccer in the afternoon?

No, she doesn't. She plays badminton.
   5. Q: What does Lucy like?
      A: She likes cheeseburgers.
   6. Q: What does Lucy want?
      A: She wants a smartphone.
   7. Q: What does Mark like?
      A: He likes music.
   8. Q: What does Mark want?
      A: He wants a digital camera.

Unit 4

Present Progressive 1

p. 26

Learn & Practice 1
A 1. is starting 2. is raining 3. are talking
   4. is cooking 5. is working 6. are playing

Learn & Practice 2
A

walk → walking	ride → riding	cut → cutting
visiting	taking	sitting
playing	dancing	getting
studying	writing	beginning
cleaning	making	stopping

B 1. siting → sitting 2. lookking → looking
   3. walkking → walking 4. rideing → riding
   5. eatting → eating

Learn & Practice 3
A 1. She's not working. / She isn't working.
   2. I'm not sitting in a cafe. / —
   3. It's not snowing. / It isn't snowing.
   4. We're not making dinner. / We aren't making
      dinner.
   5. They're not coming now. / They aren't coming now.
   6. Ann's not reading a newspaper. / Ann isn't reading a
      newspaper.
   7. He's not studying at home. / He isn't studying at
      home.

Super Writing
A 1. is sleeping 2. isn't snowing 3. am trying
   4. are making 5. are yelling 6. isn't working

B 1. isn't watching TV; is listening to music

2. aren't walking; are riding their bicycles

3. aren't studying in the library; are walking to school

4. isn't running; is swimming in a pool

C 1. She is getting up.

2. She is washing

3. She is brushing

4. She is drinking

5. She is reading

6. She is brushing

7. She is opening

8. She is going

D 1. The man and the woman aren't sitting in a cafe.
They are standing in the street.

2. The man isn't speaking on the phone.
The woman is speaking on the phone.

3. The man isn't holding a newspaper.
He is holding a book.

4. The woman isn't looking at the book.
She is looking at the man.

5. The woman isn't holding a suitcase.
She is holding her phone.

6. It isn't snowing. The sun is shining.

Review Test (Unit 1–4)   p. 32

A 1. No, I'm not hungry. I'm thirsty.

2. No, they're not good soccer players. They're good tennis players.

3. No, he's not an astronaut. He's a firefighter.

4. No, it's not expensive. It's cheap.

B 1. is raining   2. is playing   3. are swimming

C 1. speaks   2. closes   3. teaches   4. lives   5. have

D 1. Does he have a new car?

2. Do they love her?

3. Do you like movies?

4. Does Susan walk to school?

E 1. doesn't wash her face; brushes her teeth

2. doesn't drink coffee; drinks milk every day

3. doesn't play tennis; plays badminton every day

F 1. I'm not asking for a lot of money.

2. She's not listening to me.

3. It's not raining now.

4. She's not wearing a coat.

5. We're not enjoying this film.

6. You're not eating much these days.

Unit 5   p. 34

Present Progressive 2

Learn & Practice 1

A 1. Is; wearing; she isn't

2. Is; studying; she is

3. Is; cooking; he isn't

4. Are; doing; they are

Learn & Practice 2

A 1. are going (Future Plan)

2. is taking (Now)

3. are taking (Future Plan)

4. is starting (Future Plan)

5. are rushing (Now)

6. is having (Future Plan)

7. is boiling (Now)

8. is getting (Future Plan)

Learn & Practice 3

A 1. What; She; flying   2. Who; My mother; sleeping

3. What; I; reading

Super Writing

A 1. Is she standing next to a horse?

2. Is he washing his dad's car?

3. Are they painting the house?

B 1. At 9:00 she is playing badminton with her father.

2. At 11:00 she is meeting Bob and Laura at the department store.

3. At 12:00 she is having lunch with her friends.

4. At 2:00 she is going to the movie theater with her mother.

5. At 4:00 she is studying in the library.

6. At 6:00 she is eating dinner with her family.

7. At 8:00 she is doing her math homework.

C 1. Q: Is she watching TV?
A: No, she isn't. She is listening to music.

2. Q: Are they learning science?
A: No, they aren't. They are learning history.

3. Q: Is he reading a book?
A: No, he isn't. He is working on his laptop.

4. Q: Is he drinking tea?

A: No, he isn't. He is washing the dishes.

D 1. Q: Who is driving the car?

2. A: She is playing the guitar.

3. Q: Who is waiting for the train?

4. A: She is buying clothes.

5. Q: Who is sleeping in the office?

6. A: He is tasting the soup.

Unit 6 p. 40
Nouns, Articles

Learn & Practice 1

A 1. Common Noun: teacher
   Proper Noun: Nancy

2. Common Noun: city
   Proper Noun: Chicago

3. Common Noun: river
   Proper Noun: Nile

4. Common Noun: school
   Proper Noun: Yonsei University

Learn & Practice 2

A 1. a 2. a 3. an 4. an 5. an 6. a 7. a 8. a

Learn & Practice 3

A 1. boxes 2. boys 3. cities 4. foxes 5. tools
   6. benches 7. buses 8. potatoes 9. ships
   10. countries 11. ladies 12. bikes

Learn & Practice 4

A 1. teeth 2. fish 3. people 4. children 5. women

Super Writing

A

Add -s	Add -es	Add -ies	Irregular
apples	glasses	cities	people
chairs	dresses	countries	women
tables	churches	stories	men
ships	buses	ladies	fish
boats	tomatoes	dictionaries	geese

B 1. It is an elephant.

2. They are women.

3. There are five children.

4. It is a fish.

5. These are geese.

6. It is an egg.

C 1. He is a taxi driver.

2. She is an auto mechanic.

3. She is an architect.

4. He is an English teacher.

5. She is a photographer.

6. He is an electrician.

D 1. The pencils are on Maria's desk.

2. The babies are in the crib.

3. The women are living in London.

4. The tomatoes from the store look yummy!

5. The cities look great after the clean-up effort.

6. The mice are coming to us.

7. The men are looking at me.

Unit 7 p. 46
Pronouns, Demonstratives

Learn & Practice 1

A 1. She is a doctor.

2. We dance well.

3. They are twins.

4. It is white.

5. They are yellow.

6. They are on the table.

Learn & Practice 2

A 1. them 2. her 3. us 4. it 5. me 6. him

B 1. her 2. we 3. you; me 4. him 5. them 6. it
   7. them

Learn & Practice 3

A 1. This is; that is 2. This is; those are

B 1. this; it isn't 2. these; they aren't

Super Writing

A 1. she → her 2. them → it 3. us → them
   4. them → it

B 1. These are computers.

2. This is a desk.

3. These are notebooks.

4. This is a skateboard.

5. Those are paper bins.

6. That is a plant.

7. That is a sofa.

8. Those are schoolbags.

9. That is a clock.

10. Those are paintings.

C I; They; me; we; them; us; We; you; you; She; she; them

D **1**. Is that; No, it isn't. It is a schoolbag.

2. Are these; No, they aren't. They are oranges.

3. are those; They are horses.

4. Is this; No, it isn't. It is an MP3 player.

Unit 8
p. 52
Possessives

Learn & Practice 1

A **1**. her **2**. your **3**. our **4**. their **5**. his **6**. my **7**. its

Learn & Practice 2

A **1**. friend's name

2. dog's tail

3. women's shirts

4. Jane's phone

5. boys' skateboards

6. teachers' room

Learn & Practice 3

A **1**. That's mine.

2. It's hers.

3. These are yours.

4. Are those theirs?

5. Yours looks terrible.

6. That dog looks like ours.

7. I prefer our house to theirs.

Learn & Practice 4

A **1**. Q: Whose; are   A: his

2. Q: Whose; is   A: hers

3. Q: Whose; are   A: Olivia's

4. Q: Whose; are   A: mine

5. Q: Whose; is   A: theirs

Super Writing

A **1**. the children's dog

2. the girl's ice skates

3. the boys' skateboards

4. the girl's tennis racquet

5. the boy's bicycle

B **1**. Whose bicycle is that?

It's Jane's.

2. Whose T-shirt is that?

It's Ted's.

3. Whose car is that?

It's my parents'.

4. Whose shoes are those?

They're William's.

5. Whose skateboard is that?

It's Kelly's.

6. Whose binoculars are those?

They're Linda's.

C **1**. The backpack is his.

2. The laptop computer is hers.

3. The digital camera is theirs.

4. The jacket is his.

5. The guitar is theirs.

6. The hairdryer is hers.

D **1**. Those are the teacher's books.

Those are his books. Those are his.

2. That is the nurse's thermometer.

That is her thermometer. That is hers.

3. Those are the doctor's tools.

Those are his tools. Those are his.

4. That is the mechanic's wrench.

That is his wrench. That is his.

Review Test (Unit 5-8)
p. 58

A **1**. Q: Is Patty tidying her room now?

A: Yes, she is.

2. Q: Is your brother working on his computer now?

A: No, he isn't. He is having lunch.

3. Q: Are you doing your homework at the moment?

A: Yes, I am.

4. Q: Is Jane sleeping in the living room?

A: No, she isn't. She is watching TV.

B **1**. Men and women **2**. feet **3**. skies **4**. Raindrops

5. children

C **1**. she; me **2**. they; us **3**. he; her **4**. I; you

5. she; them

D **1**. Q: Whose violin is this?

A: It's Rebecca's violin.

2. Q: Whose ball is this?

A: It's the children's ball.

3. Q: Whose shoes are these?

A: They're Michael's shoes.

4. Q: Whose MP3 player is this?

A: It's Chloe's MP3 player.

E 1. He is reading a book.

2. They are seeing a movie.

3. She is playing basketball with her friends.

4. They are playing tennis.

Unit 9
Count/Noncount Nouns, Quantity Questions p. 60

Learn & Practice 1
A 1. milk 2. advice 3. furniture 4. snow 5. butter
6. tea

Learn & Practice 2
A 1. a carton of 2. three pieces of

Learn & Practice 3
A 1. any 2. some 3. a 4. any 5. some 6. any

Learn & Practice 4
A 1. many → much 2. meals → meal
3. many → much 4. much → many
5. much → many 6. many → much

Super Writing
A any; any; some; any; some; any; any; any

C 1. Q: How much milk does he drink?

A: He drinks six glasses of milk.

2. Q: How many eggs does he eat?

A: He eats five eggs.

3. Q: How many slices of bread does he eat?

A: He eats seven slices of bread.

4. Q: How many doughnuts does he have?

A: He has four doughnuts.

5. Q: How much coffee does he drink?

A: He drinks two cups of coffee.

D 1. milk 2. bread 3. butter 4. cheese 5. coffee
6. egg 7. doughnut

Unit 10
Will, Articles (Definite/Zero) p. 66

Learn & Practice 1
A 1. rain 2. be 3. get 4. visit

B 1. I will study hard.

2. She won't come to the party.

3. They won't be late

4. My mom will cook chicken for dinner

5. Bob will be a famous chemist

Learn & Practice 2
A Q: Will she become a figure skater? A: she won't

Q: Will it be sunny tomorrow? A: it will

Q: Will he get married next year? A: he won't

Q: Will people live in space colonies? A: they will

Learn & Practice 3
A 1. the 2. × 3. the 4. × 5. the 6. × 7. The
8. ×

Super Writing
A 1. Laila will drive an electric car tomorrow.

2. Laila won't go to the supermarket tomorrow.

3. Laila will help Susan move from her apartment tomorrow.

4. Laila won't take the dog for a walk tomorrow.

5. Laila will finish her project tomorrow.

B 1. She'll miss the school bus.

2. It'll become a best-seller.

3. He won't finish the race.

4. They'll win the game.

5. I won't catch my plane.

6. It'll be a thunderstorm.

C 1. the 2. a; the 3. a; a 4. a; The; a 5. ×
6. an; the; the

D 1. Q: Will they go to the movies?

A: They will paint the house.

2. Q: Will all the family be at the wedding?

A: They will be at the park.

3. Q: Will Chris wash his clothes?

A: He will play the violin.

4. Q: Will Linda hang out with her friends?

A: She will go shopping with her mom.

Unit 11

Simple Past of Be

p. 72

Learn & Practice 1

A 1. was 2. were 3. was 4. were 5. were 6. were

Learn & Practice 2

A 1. weren't 2. wasn't 3. weren't 4. wasn't
  5. wasn't 6. wasn't

Learn & Practice 3

A 1. was; it was; it wasn't
  2. Were; I was; I wasn't
  3. Was; she was; she wasn't

Super Writing

A 1. Q: Was Nadia Comaneci an artist?
     A: No, she wasn't. She was a gymnast.
  2. Q: Was Neil Armstrong a professor?
     A: No, he wasn't. He was an astronaut.
  3. Q: Was Thomas Edison a president?
     A: No, he wasn't. He was an inventor.
B 1. Destiny wasn't a singer. She was a fashion model.
  2. Bob wasn't a painter. He was a doctor.
  3. Sandra wasn't fat. She was slender.
  4. Sujin and Minho weren't teachers. They were students.
C 1. Q: was Peter last Tuesday
     A: He was at the supermarket.
  2. Q: were you and your friends last Saturday
     A: They were at the restaurant.
  3. Q: were Emma and her parents yesterday afternoon
     A: They were at the train station.
  4. Q: was Jessica last night
     A: She was at the movie theater.
D 1. weren't late 2. wasn't interesting 3. with Alex
  4. weren't in England 5. wasn't a teacher

Unit 12

Simple Past 1

p. 78

Learn & Practice 1

A 1. watched 2. didn't answer 3. rained 4 worked

5. didn't visit

Learn & Practice 2

A 1. Did they play baseball yesterday?
  2. Did we watch the movie last Saturday?
  3. Did she move to Singapore?
  4. Did it rain yesterday?
  5. Did he walk downtown yesterday?
B 1. No, he didn't. 2. Yes, it did. 3. Yes, I did.
  4. No, she didn't.

Learn & Practice 3

A 1. stayed 2. listened 3. studied 4. loved
  5. cried 6. worked 7. carried 8. washed
  9. started 10. wanted 11. stopped 12. lived
  13. planned 14. tried 15. invited
B 1. invited 2. studied 3. played 4. walked
  5. arrived 6. planned

Super Writing

A 1. Yesterday William cleaned the garage, but he didn't clean his bedroom.
  2. Yesterday William visited his uncle, but he didn't visit his grandparents.
  3. Yesterday William studied Korean, but he didn't study Japanese.
  4. Yesterday William watched a movie, but he didn't watch the news.
  5. Yesterday William listened to music on the radio, but he didn't listen to English CDs.
C 1. Did Amy talk to Tom yesterday?
     No, she didn't. She talked to Steve.
  2. Did the boy clean the house last Friday?
     No, he didn't. He washed the car.
  3. Did Kelly visit her friends last night?
     No, she didn't. She stayed at home.
D 1. Beethoven composed the 9th symphony in 1822-1824.
  2. Mother Teresa received the Nobel Peace Prize in 1979.
  3. Alexander Fleming discovered penicillin.
  4. Florence Nightingale helped the soldiers.
  5. Alexander Bell invented the telephone.
  6. Jacques Cousteau explored the oceans.
  7. Pablo Picasso painted Guernica in 1937.
  8. Valentina Tereshkova traveled in space.
  9. Walt Disney created Mickey Mouse.

Learn & Practice 1

A

Base Form		Past Form	Base Form		Past Form
buy	→	bought	come	→	came
see	→	saw	make	→	made
take	→	took	eat	→	ate
drink	→	drank	sit	→	sat
feel	→	felt	get	→	got
give	→	gave	go	→	went
have	→	had	hear	→	heard
write	→	wrote	read	→	read
sleep	→	slept	meet	→	met
find	→	found	put	→	put
fly	→	flew	speak	→	spoke

B 1. Mark spoke on his phone.

  2. Christina bought some flowers.

  3. Kelly and Betty ate lunch at the cafeteria.

  4. Tiffany went to bed early.

  5. I wrote a letter to my parents.

Learn & Practice 2

A 1. Where did you go yesterday?

  2. Why did you stay home?

  3. When did you come to this city?

Super Writing

A 1. went to the movie theater

  2. caught the bus

  3. ate cherries

  4. rode his bicycle

  5. drank green tea

B went; stayed; had; woke; helped; fed; did; went; swam; took; talked

C 1. Q: Who did Lisa meet at the restaurant?

   A: She met her friends.

  2. Q: Where did Sue go yesterday?

   A: She went to a bookstore.

  3. Q: What did Olivia buy last week?

   A: She bought a T-shirt.

  4. Q: How did Dennis get to work yesterday?

   A: He got to work by taxi.

  5. Q: What did Daniel and Tanya have for lunch?

   A: They had hamburgers.

D 1. Where did Amy and her sister go?

  2. When did Sarah come out of hospital?

  3. What did the children buy?

  4. Who had a bad day yesterday?

  5. Who left a bicycle in the garden?

  6. When did you see her?

A 1. enjoy 2. like 3. went 4. eat

B 1. any 2. any 3. some 4. any

C 1. How many 2. How much 3. How much

  4. How many

D 1. Was Alice at home yesterday?

  2. Was the party good?

  3. Was your mother a teacher?

  4. Were you a speed skater?

E 1. Yesterday, Jason walked the dog.

  2. Yesterday, Jason didn't play golf.

  3. Yesterday, Jason cooked lunch.

  4. Yesterday, Jason worked on a computer.

  5. Yesterday, Jason didn't cook dinner.

  6. Yesterday, Jason didn't watch a DVD.

F 1. coffee 2. bread 3. toothpaste 4. pizza 5. water

G 1. will study hard; won't listen to music

  2. will eat lunch at the cafeteria; won't do homework

H 1. → She got up early in the morning.

   → Did she get up early in the morning?

   → She didn't get up early in the morning.

  2. → He taught history at the university.

   → Did he teach history at the university?

   → He didn't teach history at the university.

  3. → She wrote a letter to her parents.

   → Did she write a letter to her parents?

   → She didn't write a letter to her parents.

  4. → The birds flew away to other countries.

   → Did the birds fly away to other countries?

   → The birds didn't fly away to other countries.

Learn & Practice 1

A **1.** on **2.** on **3.** under **4.** in

Learn & Practice 2
A **1.** next to / by **2.** between **3.** behind
   4. by / next to

Learn & Practice 3
A **1.** in front of **2.** across from **3.** above **4.** near

Super Writing
A **1.** behind the sofa **2.** in the box **3.** on the tree
   4. at the table
B **1.** There is a picture above the sofa.
   2. There is a dog next to the laptop. / There is a
      laptop next to the dog.
   3. There is a baby under the blanket.
   4. There are boys across from the girls. / There are
      girls across from the boys.
C **1.** 5 **2.** 4 **3.** 2 **4.** 7 **5.** 1 **6.** 3 **7.** 8 **8.** 6 **9.** 10
   10. 9
D **1.** is the pen; It's on; in front of
   2. are the gloves; They're on; behind
   3. is the shirt; It's on; under
   4. are the glasses; They're on; under
   5. is the bag; It's on; near
   6. is the torch; It's on; behind
   7. is the lamp; It's on; near
   8. are the socks; They're in; above
   9. are the trousers; They're in; below
   10. are the shoes; They're on; near

Unit 15
Prepositions of Time
p. 98

Learn & Practice 1
A **1.** at **2.** at **3.** in **4.** on **5.** on **6.** in **7.** on **8.** in

Learn & Practice 2
A **1.** When **2.** When **3.** What time **4.** When
   5. What time **6.** When **7.** What time
B **1.** When do you use this camcoder?
   2. When is the concert?
   3. When is our flight?
   4. What time do you get up?
   5. What time do you eat dinner?

C **1.** at **2.** at **3.** in **4.** in **5.** on

Super Writing
A **1.** do; in **2.** cleans; on **3.** wakes; at; in **4.** visit; on
B at; in; at; at; At; at; in; at; at; at
D **1.** What time do you eat breakfast?
   2. What time do you leave home?
   3. When do you have violin lessons?
   4. What time does the store open?
   5. When is New Year's Day?
   6. When is Valentine's Day?
   7. What day is Christmas?
   8. What day is Valentine's Day?
E **1.** They eat pizza on Fridays.
   2. I always feel tired in the morning.
   3. Linda finished high school in 1998.
   4. We don't go out at night.

Unit 16
Adjectives
p. 104

Learn & Practice 1
A **1.** old **2.** happy **3.** nice **4.** beautiful **5.** smart
   6. tired **7.** brown **8.** new

Learn & Practice 2
A **1.** Adjective: big | Noun: house
   2. Adjective: expensive | Noun: bicycle
   3. Adjective: small | Noun: villages
   4. Adjective: favorite | Noun: food
   5. Adjective: new | Noun: jacket
   6. Adjective: interesting | Noun: experience
B **1.** note **2.** light **3.** key **4.** paper

Learn & Practice 3
A **1.** expensive **2.** happy **3.** slow **4.** spicy **5.** sad
   6. strong
B **1.** Australian **2.** Brazilian **3.** English **4.** Chinese
   5. Canadian **6.** French

Super Writing
A **1.** The delicious food smells good.
   2. What is your favorite food?
   3. The elephant lives on the hot plains in Africa.
   4. There are famous pyramids in Egypt.

5. Cindy is wearing her pink dress.

B 1. Natalia isn't Spanish. She is Portuguese.

2. She isn't tall. She is short.

3. She is single. She isn't married.

4. She isn't old. She is young.

5. She isn't fat. She is thin.

6. William isn't Canadian. He is American.

7. He isn't a doctor. He is a company employee.

8. He isn't thin. He is fat.

9. He isn't short. He is tall.

10. He is married. He isn't single.

C 1. My bag is brown.

2. This ring is expensive.

3. John's house is big.

4. That insect is tiny.

D 1. baseball bat   2. car key   3. house slippers
   4. vegetable soup

E She looks happy. She has straight hair. Her hair is long.
Her hair is black. She is young.
He has short hair. His hair is curly and dark brown. He
is young, too. He seems tired. He looks
bored/sad/angry.

p. 110

Unit 17

Adverbs

Learn & Practice 1

A 1. played   2. plays   3. big   4. quietly   5. wrong

B 1. tells how   2. tells where   3. tells when
   4. tells how   5. tells where

Learn & Practice 2

A 1. heavily   2. easily   3. fast   4. quickly   5. well
   6. slowly   7. early   8. really   9. happily

Learn & Practice 3

A 1. I am always late for work.

2. They often eat fast food.

3. We are never late for school

4. They are sometimes absent from school.

5. He usually has breakfast at 7:30.

Super Writing

A 1. They work slowly.

2. She acts badly.

3. She drives dangerously.

4. Ava dances beautifully.

5. You sing loudly.

6. They teach well.

7. He drives carefully.

8. She swims fast.

B 1. Olivia usually walks to school.

2. She often takes the school bus.

3. She sometimes rides her bicycle.

4. She never goes by subway.

C 1. good; well (Adjective: good | Adverb: well)

2. fast (Adverb: fast)

3. hard (Adverb: hard)

4. fast (Adjective: fast)

5. good (Adjective: good)

6. well (Adverb: well)

D 6:00 - She always gets up at 6:00 in the morning.

6:40 - She always jogs at 6:40 in the morning.

7:00 - She always takes a shower at 7:00 in the
morning.

7:20 - She always eats/has breakfast at 7:20 in the
morning.

7:40 - She always brushes her teeth at 7:40 in the
morning.

8:00 - She always leaves for school at 8:00 in the
morning.

p. 116

Review Test (Unit 14-17)

A 1. at   2. at   3. on   4. on   5. in   6. in

B 1. quickly   2. easily   3. slow   4. careful   5. badly

C 1. John always goes bicycle riding.

2. Benjamin never collects stamps.

3. Harry often plays basketball on Monday morning.

4. She is usually at work on Sundays.

5. Andrea sometimes watches TV after work.

6. He is always in his office.

D 1. at   2. on   3. on   4. in   5. in   6. at

E 1. terribly   2. angrily   3. happily

F 1. When is the concert?

2. What time do you usually go to school?

3. When do you usually get up?

4. What time do you eat lunch?

G 1. It is under the bed.

2. He is behind the wall.

155

3. They are in the basket.

4. He is in front of the bus.

Unit 18

Helping Verbs

p. 118

Learn & Practice 1

A could; couldn't; can; can't

B 1. Q: Can Tom play the guitar? A: he can

2. Q: Could she stand on her head? A: she couldn't

3. Q: Could Kelly speak Korean? A: she couldn't

4. Q: Can Ava drive a car? A: she can

Learn & Practice 2

A 1. She may go to Mexico next year.

2. He will be late.

3. You may have a problem with your car.

4. Cities will become more crowded.

Learn & Practice 3

A 1. Can **2.** May **3.** Can

B 1. possibility **2.** permission **3.** permission

4. permission **5.** possibility **6.** possibility

Super Writing

A 1. She can't play volleyball.

2. She can eat with chopsticks.

3. She can make spaghetti.

4. She can't ride a bicycle.

B 1. He couldn't play soccer.

2. He could read comic books.

3. He could listen to music.

4. He couldn't swim.

5. He couldn't run around on the playground.

6. He could watch TV.

D 1. Can I borrow your pencil, please?

2. May I use your phone, please?

3. Can I go shopping with you, please?

4. Can I go to the party, please?

5. May I borrow the digital camera, please?

E 1. We may go out.

2. She may come tomorrow.

3. We may get an invitation.

4. My friends may visit me.

5. I may go to the movie theater this weekend.

F 1. Q: Can Bob speak French?   A: No, he cant.

2. Q: Can Sunny climb trees?   A: Yes, she can.

3. Q: Can Nancy play badminton?   A: No, she can't.

4. Q: Can Brian run very fast?   A: No, he can't.

Unit 19

Imperatives, Let's

p. 124

Learn & Practice 1

A Be quiet **2.** Don't smoke **3.** Turn off

B 1. Be **2.** Turn **3.** Close **4.** Don't **5.** Watch

6. Open

C 1. Don't open the window.

2. Please don't park in the driveway. / Don't park in the driveway, please.

Learn & Practice 2

A 1. d **2.** a **3.** c **4.** b

B 1. Let's go to the supermarket.

2. Let's not watch a movie.

3. Let's buy her a present.

4. Let's not go to the beach.

Super Writing

A 1. Please sign your name at the bottom. → instruction

2. Let's read the map. → suggestion

3. Don't move! You're under arrest. → order

B 1. Let's play **2.** wash **3.** Let's have **4.** Don't be

5. Don't move **6.** Turn on **7.** Let's not stay

8. Let's watch **9.** Close

C 1. Let's go to the beach.

2. Let's go to a soccer game.

3. Let's leave at six thirty.

4. Let's eat out for dinner.

5. Let's send Harry an email.

D 1. Please give me some more coffee.

2. Please stop in front of the bookstore.

3. Please take a rest and drink a lot of water.

4. Please close the window.

Learn & Practice 1

A 1. Is Nancy from Canada?
2. Were you at home yesterday?
3. Am I late for class?
4. Were we busy two days ago?
5. Were they in class yesterday?
6. Was Peter at home last night?

Learn & Practice 2

A 1. Q: What   A: is
2. Q: Where   A: is
3. Q: Who   A: is
4. Q: When   A: is
5. Q: How   A: are
6. Q: Why   A: are

B 1. What is she
2. What is it
3. Where were they
4. How are they

Super Writing

A 1. Q: Are they teachers?
   A: No, they aren't. They are dancers.
2. Q: Is he a police officer?
   A: No, he isn't. He is a waiter.
3. Q: Are they apples?
   A: No, they aren't. They are tomatoes.

B 1. Q: Was Napoleon a musician?
   A: No, he wasn't. He was a good leader.
2. Q: Was Leonardo da Vinci an explorer?
   A: No, he wasn't. He was a famous painter.
3. Q: Was Andre Kim Japanese?
   A: No, he wasn't. He was Korean.
4. Q: Were the Beatles French?
   A: No, they weren't. They were English.
5. Q: Was Cleopatra Brazilian?
   A: No, she wasn't. She was Egyptian.
6. Q: Was Elvis Presley an astronaut?
   A: No, he wasn't. He was a famous singer.

C 1. Where is your bicycle?
2. When is Christmas?
3. Where were they yesterday?
4. When is Halloween?

Learn & Practice 1

A 1. Does she eat vegetables every day?
2. Does he like French fries?
3. Did they get married 15 years ago?
4. Did Kathy go to school yesterday?
5. Did she visit her grandmother?
6. Did Ben talk on the phone to his friend?

Learn & Practice 2

A 1. What do penguins eat?
2. Where did they live?
3. Why did you stay home?
4. How do you get to work?
5. What does she like for dessert?

Learn & Practice 3

A 1. Who broke the glasses?
2. What fell off the tree?
3. Who took my/your wallet?
4. What made me/you happy?
5. Who lives in this house?

Super Writing

A 1. How do you go
2. Where does Sunny eat lunch
3. What time does the movie start
4. Why do you study English
5. Where do kangaroos live

B 1. Q: Did she have a fever?
   A: she didn't
2. Q: Does Peter work at the post office?
   A: he doesn't
3. Q: Did Nancy go shopping?
   A: she didn't
4. Q: Does Marco eat lunch at a restaurant every day?
   A: he doesn't
5. Q: Did he exercise on Monday?
   A: he didn't

C 1. What do you eat?
2. Who knocked on the door?
3. What happened last night?
4. Who did the dishes?
5. Who were you talking to?

6. What does this word mean?

7. What did Lisa learn?

D **1.** Who did you see?

   2. When did you see her?

   3. Where did you see her?

   4. How did she look?

   5. What did she say?

   6. What did she read?

   7. What time did she come home?

H **1.** Who did you see?

   2. Who had a bad day yesterday?

   3. How did he feel?

   4. What time did he come home?

Review Test (Unit 18–21)
p. 142

A **1.** He could play soccer, but now he can't.

   2. He could dance all night, but now he can't.

   3. He could eat a lot, but now he can't.

   4. He could walk for miles, but now he can't.

   5. He could lift heavy things, but now he can't.

B **1.** Can I borrow your dictionary, please?

   2. May I use the laptop, please?

   3. Can I invite some friends to dinner, please?

C **1.** Q: What does Lucy do after school?

    A: She does her homework.

   2. Q: What does Steve do in the afternoon?

    A: He goes skateboarding.

   3. Q: Where do they go every Saturday?

    A: They go to a seafood restaurant.

   4. Q: How do they get to school?

    A: They usually walk.

D **1.** Q: Were you tired yesterday?   A: I wasn't

   2. Q: Was Jane nervous?   A: she was

   3. Q: Are they with the dog?   A: they aren't

   4. Q: Was he at the dentist's?   A: he was

   5. Q: Is she married?   A: she isn't

E **1.** Q: Did Ava email a friend last weekend? A: she didn't

   2. Q: Did you wear a new T-shirt last weekend? A: I did

   3. Q: Did Tom buy a new CD last weekend? A he didn't

   4. Q: Did they watch a movie last weekend? A: they did

F review; Sit; Go; Relax

G **1.** Let's go to a seafood restaurant.

   2. Let's go to a movie.

   3. Let's go to the beach.

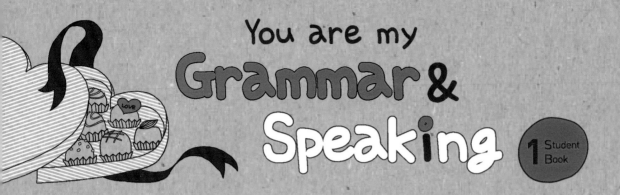

You are my Grammar & Speaking

1 Student Book

You are my Grammar & Speaking is a three-leveled grammar series that is systematically designed for young learners. This series encourages students to speak and write English accurately and fluently by providing them with a solid understanding of English grammar. This series contains the basic elements of the English grammar, writing, and speaking, through the various exercises with interesting photos and illustrations. Young learners who experience difficulties with English should find this book extremely useful. Start with the proven success of **You are my Grammar & Speaking**, and discover how easy it is to integrate grammar and communication skills.

You are my Grammar & Speaking is the following series to **Easy I am your Grammar**. **Easy I am your Grammar** (Book 1, 2, 3) is intended for learners who need to acquire the basics of grammar. **You are my Grammar & Speaking** (Book 1, 2, 3) is for learners who need to strengthen their proficiency in grammar and improve their writing and speaking skills.

Key Features

- Presentation of structures in meaningful contexts and realistic situations
- Effective 4-Step Program: Real-life Context, Learn & Practice, Super Writing, and Super Speaking
- Colorful photos and illustrations to make the series fun and interesting to learn
- Tasks to practice functions and writing used for communication
- Creative activities that stimulate speaking skills in English
- Twenty (or Twenty-one) Engaging Lessons & Review Tests

Components Also Available

- Student Book 1, 2, 3

- Workbook 1, 2, 3

For Beginners series

63740

9 788963 980911

ISBN 978-89-6398-091-1